# OF THE DEEPEST SHADOWS
# &
# THE PRISONS OF FIRE

# OF THE DEEPEST SHADOWS
# &
# THE PRISONS OF FIRE

Chimalum Nwankwo

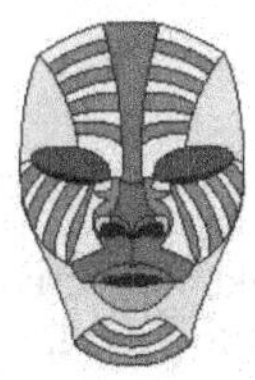

**AFRICAN HERITAGE PRESS**
**NEW YORK LAGOS LONDON**
**2010**

AFRICAN HERITAGE PRESS

NEW YORK
PO BOX 1433
NEW ROHELLE
NY 10802

LAGOS
PO BOX 14452
IKEJA, LAGOS
NIGERIA

TEL: 718-862-3262
FAX: 718-862-1440
Email: afroheritage9760@aol.com
www.africanheritagepress.com

First Edition, African Heritage Press, 2010



Library of Congress catalog number:: 2009931552

Nwankwo, Chimalum

Cover Design: Dapo Ojoade

Distributors: African Books Collective,
www.africanbookscollective.com

The characters and events in this book are fictitious. Any similarity to persons or situations is coincidental and not intended by the author.

ISBN: 978-0-9790858-2-6
ISBN: 0-9790858-2-9

# ACKNOWLEDGEMENTS

I am very grateful to the following: Sandra Grayson who first published "A Walk into the Sea" (for Walter Sisulu) and "Silent Steps" (for Funmilayo Ransome-Kuti) in *NET-WORK 2000: In the Spirit of the Harlem Renaissance*; Ntone Edjabe, editor of *Chimurenga* who first published "The Crucifixion" (for Robert Mugabe); and Major Jackson who invited me to read it at the University of Vermont African Literature Association 2009 annual conference. My gratitude to the appreciative audience which kept asking me after the reading: "Where is the book...Where is the book...?" I thank Emeka Egwuda who as an executive of the Association of Nigeria Authors, Lagos, also invited me to read "The Crucifixion" for the first time at one of their special gatherings. I am grateful to Nnorom Azuonye, editor of *SentinelPoetry.org* who first published "Bush Fire" (for Christopher Okigbo) and for choosing me as one of his Guests, and for later organizing a competition for commentary on "Bush Fire". I thank Nawal El Saadawi (*Woman at Point Zero*) who invited me to the Arab Women's Solidarity Organization conference in Cairo, Egypt, 2003, where I first read *From a Competing God* (*for George W. Bush*).Thanks to Emma Okocha, managing editor of *America Mi Dream* who persistently annoys some people by telling them that Chimalum is "the greatest".

I really greatly appreciate Okocha's insistence that I serve as an international editor and regular contributing poet for his ambitious rising magazine, *America Mi Dream*.
The poems for Malcolm X, George Bush, Tony Blair, and Rosa Parks, first appeared in *America Mi Dream*. A version of "Wedding Memory" first appeared as the lead poem in The International Library of Poetry's THE COLORS OF LIFE. Thanks also to effervescent Igbo dramatist and perspicacious critic and poet, Professor Esiaba Irobi, who in his numerous presentations refers to "Bush Fire" as the ultimate in Igbo Poetics. I am grateful also to Chido Nwangwu,

managing editor and publisher of USAfricaonline who invited me to read "Bird of Distances" as event Lead poet during the fiftieth anniversary celebrations of Achebe's *Things Fall Apart* in August 2008 at Houston, Texas.

The final version of this volume was proofed and formatted by Ms. Mia Mitchell. I am thankful to her for her assistance. How can I forget my friend, Professor Robert Levine who turned over a few words so much that I nearly cried from the pain from his meticulous critical eye? I am grateful for his patient assistance in my revisions.

I do not believe that this list of acknowledgements would be considered complete without mentioning my publishers, African Heritage Press for their faith in the quality of my creativity, and their continued support, especially Sir Basil Njoku whose appreciation of my work in African poetry remains a special kind of inspiration. I am grateful for all their sacrifices.

Finally, a special thanks for the University of Nigeria, my alma mater. On Friday, May 13, 2005, the Faculty of Arts in collaboration with the Departments of Theater Arts and English, in association with the indefatigable Greg Mbajiorgu and the South East Association of Nigeria Authors arranged for a packed University Arts Theater reading and reception where many of the poems in ***Prisons of Fire*** were first heard. Their very kind reception remains unforgettable; and their very moving, and humbling applause still rings in my ears...

## CONTENTS

## Poet's Preface: Of the Deepest Shadows and the Prisons of Fire

In the Igbo country where I grew up, the "science" through which the environment was read and governed was as magical and mythical as it was real. The great criss-cross of traffic between the living and dead was understood and accepted. The liminoid hours, when the Spirits supposedly broke out from the *deep shadows* to be part of human activity, was particularly palpable in terms of its heavy mysterious silence. Elders at such hours, between 9am and noon, would usually have left for work on the farms. Only the most aged were at home with baby sitters and little ones. The silences were punctuated by the cry of birds or the various chirrups of insects, maybe a plaintive lullaby from a neighboring homestead. If you were living there, you wished for those punctuations to be frequent. It was a naked daylight silence more forbidding, more potently vibrant than the robed silence of the pall of night. As a little boy in that environment, I felt things and promptings from unknown presences. What I felt is what powers today the private adult myths through which I read my destiny and through which I attempt to scratch at the veneers of the *deeper shadows*, or the inscrutable veil which swathes human destiny.

In this volume, references to *deep shadows* should be understood in terms of a characterization that is inviolably real and so privately experiential that evolving a counter alternate reality impairs an understanding of the poetry. The envisioned world is already an alternate reality and another super-text or meta-text *will* only mar, and not help.

The more I contemplate the nature of our universe, the more convinced I become regarding my personal suspicions about the *deeper* character of our universe. The recent discovery of the *planemos,* the twin planet-like bodies at the fringes of our solar system, indicates all manners of presences beyond our limited physical senses. We have been living with these *planemos* orbiting around each other probably these billions of years without knowing they are out there. Thanks to the burgeoning eyes of Astrophysics, we are able to determine that one of the bodies is seventeen times the size of Jupiter, and the other four times the size of Jupiter. I remain mindful in my awe, that these bodies, like our dear Earth, are in the middle of nowhere in the cosmic scheme.

I am fascinated by the fact that the gravitational forces which hold those bodies are invisible forces which not even the probes of science have been able to identify physically or with affirmable tactility. Similarly, I am compelled to suspect that there are also probably other invisible forces and presences, ethereal or metaphysical morphs around us undertaking duties and responsibilities beyond the comprehension or calibrations of our ordinary limited mortal or physical capabilities. There is a grid being firmed or firmed into place and sustained by what we cannot see and what we cannot know and do not know. The authors of that grid are the forces I periodically associate with the *deep shadows* in my newer writings and in this book of poetry. Atheistically, it is possible to laugh at the tale of various incomprehensible phenomena, or question and ridicule the numinous and the impalpable because of the absence of the rational foundations with which to deal with such. That is understandable in our scientific age, and as understandable as it is, the question of an *existential why* remains unsatisfied by the *physical what* which our senses have been able to or are able to deal with in relation to the universe or the cosmic system.

The references to *the prisons of fire* are to the mysterious forges, negative or positive, encasing every being or object in the respective universes of our existence. I read all that in the same manner in which the cosmic system is encased by the larger fire which births the various bodies out there, whether they be *planemos* or the older formations which we are still struggling to understand.

This volume celebrates *mostly*, big people with big hearts who have deeply touched the hearts and destiny of Africa and Africans. It also touches or defines a few insensitive hearts I have encountered in my tramping around the planet, especially Mary Ellen Tombstone, a pathetic woman, whose weird behavior affected my destiny in a very strange way. I initially read the encounter as evil and negative but on deeper reflection learned to read the whole experience as part of my proverbial great *deep dance, part of the dance of planets!* There are a few poetic cynical strikes at specific or vague historical moments, shadowy characters and assorted provocateurs. In the swirl of my thoughts and contemplations, I remember , among many occurrences the betrayal and murder of Patrice Lumumba, and Fidel Castro's soldiers whose self-less assistance to Africa ensured Angolan independence. I would not equally forget Oprah Winfrey for sending un-forgettable gladness to South Africa girls , an event that drew tears from my eyes.

As already indicated this volume, deals with Africa, thus I have found it appropriate to end it with a tribute to Chinua Achebe, inscribed under ORBIT OF LIGHT. How can any serious person contemplating black destiny in our time skip the epochal relevance of *Things Fall Apart*?

I must state that I do not find it an exciting honor to be compared with Christopher Okigbo. Okigbo was a great pioneer African poet whose poetry played well for his time. We are playing today in an arena and *zeitgeist* so very far away from that time. The lazy critic and the aspiring poet should come to terms with that reality. Forgive me if I emphatically say that I do not find a comparison as flattering as some younger poets and some other people think, at this stage in my career. The last word, so far, on that issue was courageously presented by Austin Akpuda at the Harvard conference on Okigbo's poetry. My politics of culture and groupthink and the intrinsic Igbo pragmatism which goes with it, speak, I believe, quite eloquently, for my politics of art and life. That is so far away from the politics and practice which defined Okigbo's life and poetry. What I call *groupthink* is the way of the world, and I do not believe it will ever change as long as we live in spaces called "nations".

Groupthink comes before any pretensions to globalism. Until there is a playing field that is satisfactorily cosmic and culturally encompassing, speaking toward notions of globalism will remain as phony as the old ragged discredited tale of *universalism*. To reverse that clear order suggesting a universal harmony of all cultures is spurious and politically disingenuous. It will amount to trying to stand the world on its head as Igbo elders say. Nothing can be before what I regard as a pre-conditional ontological ecumenism. It is on such plains that I part ways with other African bards and thinkers, past and present.

I am indebted in much of my recent thoughts to the encounter with the seminal work of late Sir Fred Hoyle whose astrophysical explorations triggered a lot of what later followed in the readings of space by modern Physics. I am equally indebted in my thoughts to the curious wisdom of my Igbo ancestors whose suspicions of the nature of our *more immediate* universe led to all kinds of myths which I have found very useful in the great marriage between what the physicists say and what Igbo folklore imparts to my consciousness.

If the religious and the mystical make references to alien alternate spaces characterized as heaven or hell and so forth, and you, readers, accept and indulge them, contemplate without haste the notion of the *deep shadows* and the various *prisons of fire* which you will encounter in this volume of poetry. If your love for somebody is not a prison, certainly your hatred is, and indeed any powerful ideas which hold you in helpless thrall. Contemplate also without haste the relationship between the new world of this poetry and the echoes of the world you encountered in a previous volume, (*The Womb in the Heart*).. *Appropriately, the timbre of this new collection comes to you with many different measures, with different takes of our world...Be reminded, finally, even if irritably, that I am an Igbo poet writing in English...!*

# PRAYERS

# Spirit of all Grammar

Severe teacher of the blind and foolish
Of all the forlorn and godforsaken
I am in the desolate prison of fire
I flap blindly in the rafters of life
I am a little bat in a nameless homestead
Fate has brought me down on my knees

Spirit of all grammar known and unknown
I salute you and your mighty agents
Whatever is done in your deepest absence
Must be repeated in your great presence

I must leave ample spaces for your absence
For the unfailing strokes of your crimson pen
The proof of absence is that there was something there
Which is not there that ought to be there

I must leave ample spaces for you
I must leave for you the punctuations
Because you alone deserve and have the power
I must leave for you the rounding off of characters
The little things which grip the lazy and the foolish

I must leave for you the embellishments
The final size and shape of things

A poet's word is a nuptial of the mind and the world
Be in your absence like the father of the bride
Without whose blessings nothing will be
From the rehearsed embraces to wine and cheer
Be in your absence the festival spirit
Without whose blessings feasts turn riot

Spirit of all spaces empty and full
Better empty spaces than detonations of bitter wills
Better empty spaces than throngs of phrases
Gleaming and trenchant like murderous marchers
Screaming in desperation for this or for that
Better empty spaces than a germ of anarchy
Waiting carelessly like an ominous line
Like the bomb on the belly of a plane for war
With deaths certain potency hidden in steel
In the broad smile of a fiery sun

Punctuations will limit the power of your pen
And warn the world of wasps and thrones
So I will not consider the use of one

Let these freedom lines stand condemned

Like the armed robbers picked up in ruthless haste
Pinioned to the stakes for the crude squad bullets
When callous dictators and their crazy cohorts
Bankrupt in action and bankrupt in ideas
Wobble their countries to death and despair
Like jaded vehicles on broken wheels

There is something terrible in all punctuations
It distracts from the venom and focus of the killer
It gives character to what does not need it
It warns that thinkers pause before they act
They scout direction and weigh consequences
Hand on scabbard the masquerade pauses
Perhaps to hear the ancestor's secret whispers
Before the ugly sight of blade and blood
But that was in the age of strange masquerades
And this is the age of bloodless strikes

Punctuations will always betray order
The secret memories of all the shallow graves
All the graves of those who dared
Whether the regime is civil or just brutal
They will always betray and coldly reveal
The deliberation for the sanitized murder
For one national game or hollow past-time
The velvet spread over the greed of power

Must know no wrinkle or one betrayal

Punctuations could suggest cancellations
And the desired hesitations of a moral heart
Punctuations could suggest the growth of a soul
The notion of balances between the right and just
Punctuations could suggest the probe of all roots
The secrets at the great base of all the cosmos

I know these words will truss me up on the stake
Like the armed robber of a benighted world
Awaiting the cancellation of a dictator's nod
Do not bite your crimson pen in thought
Stop thinking and sear me with those deft strokes
Care little about the prison of fire
Where survivors may fight fire even more with their teeth
And curse the flames of a hapless world
Lit by some clowns crowned by the blind
And if by chance you remember my roots
Name them scrolls from a dead man's shelves
Dumb bells pealing in the deepest of nights...

# Heart of the Moon and Sun

## (*Prayer for Tyrants*)

1

How nice to walk before the face of each other
Where a presence is no testament of war
How nice to walk before the face of each other

The moon and the sun do not always mind
The to and fro of all the deep dances
The veneer sloughed from the walk of snakes

The dignity of the sun is from not minding
And without minding the moon takes and gives
They do not shut their glares and glows
Their hearts are large and open hearths
Their premises too are open avenues
They have no walls and seize no prisoners
And how to keep prisoners they do not know
Their premises are always open avenues
How I long for the heart of the moon
And how I long for the heart of the sun

Ah ... heart of noble giants

How your seat of courage could have helped
The trembling heart of the mask of power

2

The tyrants live in fear behind iron gates
The marble walls are prisons of fire
Every inch is covered with peepholes
The walls wear like the tyrant's restless head
Razor tiaras and electric spikes

The horizon is a stretch of languor and waste
Where the tyrant's eyes raise jungles of demons
The light of the moon is gracious and generous
But the tyrant's heart does not feel its glow
It is a world of ghouls and a world of dragons
Dancing to the music of the tyrant's heart
It is a wild world of stalking bull thunders
Leaping and snarling from the tyrant's head
It is a whirling world of vengeful shadows
Roaring like breakers to the palace gates

The sun's respite is a sea of mirages
Shaking with sharks drunk with the smell of blood
The sun rises in the morning with brushes of gold
But the tyrant's eyes are a veil of cobwebs

And the twilight glory of softest colors
Wastes away into the wells of dusk
And when forest denizens chant for the world to sleep
The tyrant groans under the hoofs of nightmares
Between the heart and the head of the restless one
A deck of cards with a rule of cheats

Ah ... heart of noble giants
Should I ever seize the throne of a tyrant
To douse for a moment our prison of fire
Give me the courage to live with open gates
Behind low walls of ferns and flowers
Give me the power of the moon and the sun
Give me the wisdom for the shared passages
Give me the spirit of all open spaces
The spirit of the arena of the deepest dances
Where motions do not mean testaments of war
Where boulders roll among the galaxies
Like pillows of feather and soft cotton balls...

# Fire & the Deep Shadows ...

# Prisons of Fire

The spirits draped the lands beyond the spyglass
But the people draped themselves with other things

God put his hands inside the palm leaves and waves
Every day the waves but no one sees the leaves

The Goddess and the spirits of the river cry with fullness
The glory of their cries bounces off the water surface

The cries meet with the eyes of the sun asking
What devil cotton grows wool in the ears of these people?

The eyes I see have no iron cataracts
They do not have the flaming glaucoma

And yet they do not see the prison walls
With its great flames growling like lions

*Prisons of fire and prisons of fire*
That is the howling song of their strange world...

# Of the Deepest Shadows

Those who live beyond the deepest shadows
Who do not know of the great deep dance

The dance of women under the udala tree
Do not know the path of sweetest milk

Between the root and bole of life's coconut
Where luscious fruits are swaying in the breeze...

# Earth Call

I was the field
Left fallow for the planting

And you did not come

The rains fell
And the earth was wet

And you did not come

The field turned sand
And the wind dirged

And you did not come

A sandstorm came with music
And specters danced in cyclones

And you did not come

Who will bear the blame?
And whose head the ashes?

When my world becomes
One great prison of furious fire
Where our bellows blow with closed eyes
Less than a speck of what has glowed
Less than the specks of what petered out
We live inside this envelope of fire
Where we do not man the bellows

We live among ashes over ashes
Inside and around our prison of fire
Less than whatever will come burning
For what will come burning knows the road
The signs of traffic in all orbits

# Calling the Night

Blanket of the eddy of all distances
Festival color after failures all victories

I weave my mantle from your sheen of power
My laughter helps my veil of mysteries

The stars gave me your deep velvet robe
To cover the cold moon glow in my heart

When the forests of life part in the morning
I read your power there before my passing

When the moon grows large in my heart
I know it is fear alone that I should fear

So much lurks there in the funereal air
So much, very few can see without aid

Wine surges in the notes of our bristling flutes
In the beats of our hearts in the booming drums

I have already trapped your sacred energies

I have the terror of your color in my songs

For storms and for the peoples stones of pain
I ask for the forehead of the king of evil

For the sling of justice and the poison of sorrow
For the anger loaded in the futile gonads

Of those rapists gone mad from the agony of want
In a land where vines may well sprout from sand

But for the wiles of all the great robber barons
Sitting over the people's yams with guns

Pirate guns from the old slavers arsenals
Guns burnished for new seas and new farms

New slaves on different new farms with lords
Dancing drunk before golden mirrors

I am no match to the madness of the times
Without fear for demons and no fear of the gods

It is either this voice from a dingy prison
Or parcel bombs and killers from the dark

# Fire

I live inside our envelope of fire
Of what we count or cannot count

The meteors come  blaze and go
The boulders cool and roll away
The planets bide their time in time
Soldiers and sentinels of the great bellows

They must stay for life or death
The stars among us and the black holes too
We all stand fixed in our single orbits
Bearing in us all our tiny little fires

This great envelope this prison of fire
Ethereal warders serve their strange delights
Stoking us with the bellows of their meals
Some will glow as comfort gospels
And some are merely excrescences

Where is the music from all the bellows?
The sun speaks always to the moon
And the moon speaks always to the earth

And always the tides rise and ebb in the great dialog

Perhaps one day the prison walls will fall
And we shall learn to speak together
And mark the orbits with our little glows
And be together lords of the envelope
Manning our bellows of fire together.

# The War

The eye of the sun has caught them inert
They lie naked with their cannibal paws

A fire is raging from homestead to homestead
For water the cry is for buckets of blood

The blood of sacrifice is what their heart's desire
But the blood of their people is what they give

If the parents do not kill the children today
The children in time will soon kill the parents

All fratricides are not from gun and long knives
A weedy village square is always good enough

What war is worse than homesteads at war?
With enemies everywhere like invisible gates

# Mongers Anthem

The coward chooses war for the velvet carpet
Which is the way of the tender footed ones
It works for those whose minds cannot go
Over the coal fires of the beasts inside
Where buildings will not stand on sand
Because the head does not know where to begin

Perhaps animals can bluster to heaven
But it will not be the heaven of the schooled spirit
It will be there where dross is flowers
Where mirages stand like rock or steel
The gold from the spires of drunken dreams
The fortunes from opiates which poverty brews
When hope is a barren tree in the dreamer's world
Before I could read the chalk of my father
Under the roof ringed by *ogilisi* trees
When guests staggered in from the rain and cold

I answered the gongs of battle without a thought
I had not seen the incense swirl around blood
I could not read the message of bodies suddenly still
When the hush runs like a stream into the deep dance
And all steps are measured and weighed for their values
For the rhythm of their beats in the dance of planets

# Memory Poem

*(of Biafra and its prison of fire)*

Then it was not about their sisters lost
Nor was it about their precious mothers
Nor of any kind of kith and kin
Not their lands which became highways

Those who applauded the rape and carnage
Could not think of their own mothers crying
They looked for the law in the barrel of guns
And in the ugly blades of trenchant knives

Lost in the agony of a nameless hate
The gropes held me like a giant spider

Those who could save one looked elsewhere
For they did not know who one's mother was

And the desire for rape glowed too in their eyes
With its embers crackling in the bush fire there

Wild love lit a bonfire for their many hearts

The forests inside let the beasts emerge

A passion rocket went into the sky
Firing disasters and the race for life

*********

O sad memory of wanton blood
What fixed firm the dynamo of such life
What sad memory of wanton hate

The whole world heard its river gurgle
And no desert of power could drink it up

Pain always frothed like fresh palm wine
In the morning its alcohol was always there
Evening shared its smoldering powers

The people ran life like holy drunkards,
Drunkards holy from the blood of their kin...
Questing for cries lost in the wilderness
Their divided families wracked their hot heads
They wondered about their wanton memories
When the spirits blew at the bellows of their pain...

# Comrade

1

Your distancing can only give you high walls
And the strange solace of a prison of fire.
Leader, you have acquired a brand new accent
Your taste for food and wine have changed
So too your shoes and massive clothing
We felt the cold winds of the harmattan together
The rain broke in torrents through our ragged rafters
We all that time had no place to hide

When fearless snakes hunted for rats in our rafters
I watched them with you in bated breath
And when we went to bed together at night
We shared one smelly pillow in fear

Will the robbers break through the bamboo fence
Left tottering by the tired termites?
Will we see together the morning sun
When the walls fall off this prison of fire?

2

Today the barbed wire stands over you

A prison of fire behind a cement wall
Your iron gate defies a battering ram
But where is the harmattan of your fine memory

What do you do with the memory of our past
When you lift your wine flutes with your new friends
And clink your golden cutlery together

Do you tell them that you do not know me
You who were with me in the cold harmattan
When the elephant of poverty was stomping over us?
And the shallow graves of enemies dogged our every step

The past remains like the breath of tank killers
With the poverty of our kinsfolk looking like grenades
From where this steel wall of silent moments
With all the missiles of our common memories
Whistling in menace with our every breath

What market stocks this velvet purring
With which you power your grand new voice
Which calms and sedates like a flawless diviner?
What powers protect you from this prison of fire...?

# The Dog Barks for You

*(for the one who lives in fear of criticism)*

Stalwart and leader of the people
We who also live in this prison of fire

Hear with you the dog's bark in the wilderness
Hear with you what the enemy will not hear

The dog is barking for us in the wilderness
The anger of bared teeth is not for the wilderness

The barking of the dog is unknown to our enemies.
Beyond the walls of this prison of fire

Stalwart and leader of the people
Listen to the anger of the dog in the wilderness

The anger of the dog is not for your throat
The dog does not bark for your blood and bones

The wilderness will not reap from the barking dog
The enemy will not reap from the dog barking

Stalwart and leader of the people
The anger of the dog is gold for your kingdom

The dog barks for the goodness of your kingdom
Because stalwart and leader of the people
The anger of the dog is gold for your kingdom...

# SACRED SPACES

## **Ibo Landing**. (*The memory of a visit*)

I spent one deep night there at Ibo Landing
And I heard the old voice of the sea whisper
Of the people wailing without graves in the sea
Of memories lost over today's empty dins
Of people who knew how death itself cowers
When the dying hold their heads high and say
*The Igbo name was not even spelt right*

In that deep deep night too at Ibo Landing
Those who walked into the sea knew well
They could seize the great banner from time
And plant their names in the furrows of the sea
And say what no master's order can alter
With blows from embers and whips from fire
*The Igbo name was not even spelled right*

They heard the huge flames of a prison of fire
Even before they left the deck of their ship
They heard flames crackling with lips of hide
And the searing sizzles from cascades of tears
What they heard was in the voice of the sea
What will thunder through today's marble hearts?
*The Igbo name was not even spelled right*

You and your children have seen Ibo Landing
The nights have neither smoke nor wind in its breath
Did you wonder there why the sea still whispers
With no sound of wails or chains in the air
The night has neither smoke nor wind in its breath
Over the velvet tarmac time rolled over the sea
*The Igbo name was not even spelled right*

*When the sea walks into all your silences*
*And whispers in the voice of whose energy is finished*
*Listen with care and take the message softly*
*The Igbo name was not even spelled right*

I do not know why I went to Ibo Landing
To feel the weight of time on my shoulders
To have my head bowed with the load of silences
To link my hands with other tired hands
And hear the old voice of the sea whisper
In the voice of one whose energy is finished
*The Igbo name was not even spelled right*

I ask you who today go to Ibo Landing
Why do you bow your heads there at Ibo Landing
And why do you link your hands together
And break down there the walls of your silences
Do you know why always the sea whispers

In the voice of one whose energy is finished
*The Igbo name was not even spelled right*

The sea will call us again tomorrow
Tomorrow the children of our children will go there
And they will hear too the old voice of the sea whisper
A chained agony wrestling with the waves of time
In the voice of one whose energy is finished
What the slaves heard when they walked into the sea
*The Igbo name was not even spelled right*

You know what those who walked into the sea knew
And the sea will always speak in that same voice
The sorrow of the surf ripples down the horizon
For sea and surf know too what the Igbo slaves knew
Is that not why the sea always whispers
In the voice of one whose energy is finished
*The Igbo name was not even spelled right*

You Igbo who go to Ibo Landing today
The slave ship sailed into the bowel of time
No sliver remains on its watery memory
Why do you today go to Ibo Landing?
Is it just to hear the old voice of the sea whisper
In the voice of one whose energy is finished?
*The Igbo name was not even spelled right*
*The Igbo name was not even spelled right...*

# SPECIAL HEARTS

# Walking into the Sea

## (*for Walter Sisulu*)

1

I know the burning bush offers us little
Because of the rising rage of omnivores

But Walter Sisulu saw much more
*I will go singing was the song of his heart*

With the terror of fangs now everywhere
From the warmest hearth to the sacred grove

Tumult has eaten the heart of silences
There are everywhere tent-poles of blood

But Walter Sisulu saw much more
*I will go singing was the song of his heart*

**2**

Do not take your bucket under the eaves
The sound on the roof is a rain of blood

Do not wander toward the old village spring
The silver sand glows with the radiance of death

But Walter Sisulu saw much more
*I will go singing was the song of his heart*

Do not seek the shade of the great iroko
The old iron roots sit on the cotton and sand

My dreams are tortures of vanishing fruits
No name frits from the vanishing trees

But Walter Sisulu saw much more
*I will go singing was the song of his heart*

Passing like the gods from this prison of fire
Like the last sweet music of a great festival

When flutes in the breeze wail ever so softly

After the thunder of drums and stamping of feet
After the ecstasy from the blaze of transition

The braids of wails with the laces of delight
Strangely touched by some strained memories

Walter Sisulu has gone on marching
*I will go singing was the song of his heart*

Walter Sisulu embraced Apartheid prisons
Like the noble black slaves did old Ibo Landing

Life is life when life is without fear
The prison of fire breaks at the sound of that song

*Walter Sisulu! Walter Sisulu!*
Why did those demons tremble at your name

3

My sister's heart is the domain of vultures
My brother's limb is the sinew of jackals

My mother forgets the nights of moon glow
My father begs in the open for offal

But for Walter Sisulu who saw much more
*I will go singing was the song of his heart*

It is a marriage of the most wicked spirits
When nights of terror marry days of evil

The miracle dwells there in the triumphant roars

In the approvals of the complacent silences

In the coronations of the bloody chieftains
In the rains of stars when an angel crashes

The burning bush offers no shelter no shade
Because of the rising rage of omnivores

Walter Sisulu did not blink at the demons
With chains on ankles and chains on wrists

Just like the noble slaves at old Ibo Landing
Who saw all the demons and did not blink

Walter Sisulu stared through fire and smoke
*I will go singing was the song of his heart*

4

*Walter Sisulu! Walter Sisulu!*
When the storms rise over the highest iroko

And the sky is howling pieces of glass
I will walk calmly into the deepest blue sea

And let the sea turn into molten magma

A boiling Jupiter come hurtling down my head

*Walter Sisulu! Walter Sisulu!*
All those who go singing like you

I will invoke all the slaves at Ibo Landing
I will call your name like the early morning cock

I will face the teeth of all the omnivores
I will not blink at the terror of their eyes

I will go singing like Walter Sisulu
*Walter Sisulu! Walter Sisulu!*

The voice of your soul will be my guide
My music the chains from the limbs of slaves

Into freedom's arms and the wings of light
I will smash the gates of the prisons of fire

Like an arrow straight into the heart of the sun
I will go singing like Walter Sisulu...

# When The Soul Train Parks

## (*Song for Rosa Parks* )

The last soul train has parked smoothly
And the roses are there now for Rosa Parks
Inside the big hall of the great ancestors
Blazoned on the vase is 9053
And it is a vase of burnished gold
And the great ancestors look at the vase and smile
Heaven sees Rosa's name and smiles
And the Earth sees it too and smiles

Before the last soul train parks for you
And from across the great seven rivers
The thunder of drums begin to recede
Earn my friend your great vase of gold
When the right thing stands before your face

In the sudden morning before your travels
Take heed and earn your vase of gold
At noon or the dead of the deepest night
Take heed and earn your vase of gold
From all over our prisons of fire
Take heed and earn your vase of gold
Let red embers crackle with giant flames

Take heed and earn your vase of gold
Earn the smile of the great ancestors
And the great smile of all our greatest people
When the last soul train parks there for you

When the last soul train parks there for you
Let us hear your name and smile
Before the halls of the great ancestors
With no phony angels standing there
Where Rosa already has arrived in style
And the great hall glows with love and pride
And Rosa has arrived in shining style
With sunny smiles greeting the name of Rosa
And all the ancestors leading the chorus
Proud to bear the vase of gold
Because the vase is great which marks Rosa's life

What else would you ever want, my friend
When you arrive in style like Rosa has done
All ready with your vase of burnished gold
When the last soul train parks for you
With no phony angels standing there?
In the light of the great smile of all the people
What else would you ever want, my friend
After the shining smile of the great ancestors
Cheering you and your vase in style
When the last soul train parks for you?

# Memorial Poem

## (*for Martin Luther King jnr*)

Outside the house of your great dream
I hear the tattered sounds of clashing melodies
Worse than your marchers' clashes with the law
Not songs of your dream and the forbidden pathways
Not songs of the palace walls for the master's revels
Palaces from which bones and crumbs sailed to us
With stones from the master's own dreams of power
Songs of ribaldry celebrating the body
Songs that have no deals with the head
Songs of orgies and of wild celebrations
The celebrants are thumping and they are singing
Your dream is marriage with the white princesses
Your dream is strolling through the halls of power
Being drunk with the aroma of the food is now sufficient
And the celebrants are oohing their senses to death
Triumphant songs coo of what to do to my baby
It is a dream world of gold and dizzying diamonds
And there is no sun where cold freezes the bones
And the singers help the growing prisons of fire
Where traps spring from the prisoner's own fingers

Because the soul of the machine is what the fingers know
Beyond what to do with my baby tonight
Little of the poverty at each turn of the road tomorrow
Songs of silken sneakers tasseled in glitz
Gold and diamonds bought from wily usurers

We live inside the great house of your dreams
We live where your name is a sign on the walls
A sign in the house of only blind people
Clouds where empty rituals rule the air
And your name is now fetish or something remembered
Your name is like the story of a ruddy Red Sea
The ruddy color conceals what to know of the water
The quiet ripples will not yield the secrets of the deep
The deep alone knows how the slaves mastered the waves
The deep knows too why the assailants called off the chase
Perhaps the assailants were part of the long tale of storms
Perhaps in this tale of assailants and the tale of slaves
The story of this house tucks its great foundations

But we must tell the tale of storms to the children
For the cold wind to touch the smiles of their cheeks
For the crash of trees to halt their careless laughter
For the wails of broken wills to strike their hearts like
knives

For their own wills to grow tendons when new winds blow
For them to learn the silenced story of our lost shivers
Because our shivers will prepare them for their own shivers
For the cold winds of death from the heels of horses
So that if it storms again we will remember how the roof was fixed

There is singing and drumming and dancing on roof tops
The singing and drumming and dancing drowns the dream
The noise over your name is like the noise after the storm
The noise drowns the wail from the storms of your blood
The noise muffles the voice which broke the iron gates of power
The sound of the waves which broke the dykes of blood
Is there in the sounds which my baby hears tonight

We did not know about the threats of death
The threats which dogged our lives from birth to death
Through the shadow of summers inside our long winters
We did not know about the journey of the underground
We who are on the boulders carved form your stolid heart
We who are on the dizzying mountain top of your dreams
We who did not know where the journey began
We who have forgotten the tears of the deepest nights
Tears of the innocents whose blood meant nothing
To the icy whips of power and the red greed of hate

Which flowed through the rivers of the masters heart
We who still do not know or understand the great question
We who deny the potency of the great questions
Which neither gods nor humans could answer for our pains
What limbered out of the languid limbs of Langston Hughes
We who only hear of the dead rumbles of the exodus
We who did not see the dust from the pursuers horses
We who cannot tell whether the sea parted or did not part
Because we do not know the story's peaks or its valleys

We do not know whether our dance is worth your name
We do not know whether our genuflections is worth your name
The value of your name or the worth of our genuflections
We are riding on the boulevards of the world on the waves of jazz
And of the blues the ancestors patented from the kingdom of heaven
On the waves of such melodies that could come only from distilled blood
Blood distilled from pain and horror without measure
Those supple waves salted now by your voice and your heart
Have lost the sacred beats of the great waterfalls
Which thundered down from the mountains of your great spirit

To the valleys where we waited like starved supplicants
Waiting for the salving salvation of the final rapture

Charlatans have gone to place wreaths by your cenotaph
Recruiting acolytes from cynics and family   turn coats
Those whose hearts are   troves of whips of blood
Time truly pelts stones at the widows of stalwarts
Secure behind the iron gates of the house of the dead
Lewd gestures pass without the whisper of an ant...

# Silent Steps

## (*for Funmilayo Ransome-Kuti*)

Elephant country pounds the earth
And there are tremors on all shores

The oceans snarl with lips of death
And in froth and in wrath furling waves

Heat compels the trembling mountain
The fiery breath of stoppered places

Nothing on earth speaks of the molten fires
Silent in wait in the belly of the earth

We are ransoms in our prisons of fire
But no silent steps can ever pass us

Lioness, see the ears of the forest
Standing for ever erect at your passing

You were the zephyr of the high grass
The grass swayed always at your passing

2

You knew lioness, how power speaks always
Most lethally without blast or horror

Like the very silent voice of flowers
Like dew on leaves in the early morning

Your heart serrated our prisons of fire
And the nation saw your lightning streak

You tore through the darkness of our sad lives
You quaked the poles of the Union Jack

You touched the spirit of Margaret Ekpo
Who took your baton to the women of Aba

They were rioters and fiery women
With hearts too stolid for Lord Lugard's grave

Hearts with tapers from Harriet Tubman
And the deathless truths from Sojourner Truth

Quiet women who knew men and women
Who stoked foundries for great iron bolsters

Bolsters for boundaries bolsters for the nation
And strong new shelters from our prison of fire

Fires from the great lands christened as colonies
Weakened with brands of cross and swords

3

Elephant country pounds on earth
And there are tremors on all shores

The lioness claims its paws from spirits
And treads the jungles in silent gaits

The cubs owe you, lioness, your silent paws
For the fever of freedom in the sojourner's heart

Baking everywhere in the prisons of fire
Close to the hearth or the distant wilderness

Time is silent always and forever
And winners travel along in silent steps

Silent steps like lightning streaks
Are great thunders waiting to confirm

The serrated dark walls of our troubled skies
The noise after the spark of detonation

The freedom of the air on the face of suffering
Ashes in the wind from our prisons of fire

4

Where are the soldiers who wanted you dead
Their names have tarnished from your acrid sweat

You who knew the silent power of water
Over the naked power of the iron rod

You whose ancestors gave palaces of gold
And you opened its gates for the masses to share

You, lioness, whose name was like your steps
A bristling terror before the seats of evil

A silent joy from the shelter of spirits
Was communion joy for the hearts of warriors

Silently, lioness you rode the high grass
The wind presses its thumb on all our memories

Silently, the little chicken runs in a dance
With the mystic grace of all chosen souls

The crash always belongs to the angry chaser
Like the ungainly fall of a lumbering beast

The master's lash outlasts his stolen names
Like the spoor of animals forever in the wind

We who remember Lord Lugard's golden grave
Will remember always the source of the gold...

# The Heart of 46664

## (for *Nelson Mandela*)

*Ritual animal*
*Gift of the spirits*

They put him away at the place of rocks
Where the ocean sang its song of dolphins

Crimson melodies will not stop the rain
When all skies know the burden of the clouds

The dolphins always learn more than their masters
The scald of baptism turns tendon into steel

Grace will always break rocks forever
And his tenure was a show of dazzling dolphins

The world heard all the demon prayers
It was for his heart to turn to rags

It turned to sacred robe in Robben Island
And the robe broke rocks for all the world

Each piece of broken rock
Gave birth to living flint;
Light from flames in a prison of fire

The flames gave voice to lips of pain
It was a marriage of garnered agonies
With nuptials at all the four corners of the world

For the holy messengers of pregnant skies
It was a show of dazzling dolphins
And crimson melodies did not stop the rain

Though the thunder of his grunt
Was heard around the world

Under a grove sheltered by a canopy of souls
His anger ran quietly like a cool village stream

His anger did not melt into the hoofs of horses
To gallop into the deep night of clouds of hate

For the storm and all the thunders of the heart
The spirits gave sages the gift of silence

The dignity of the white swan on the pacific lake
To water the parched meadows of a broken heart

Now who does not know the train of the storm
Will only see the eye of its blood red fury

*Ritual animal*
*Gift of the spirits*

The flames of your hallowed heart had no match
No match had those flames in that prison of fire

2

*Ritual animal*
*Gift of the spirits*

His blood watered a grove in Robben Island
The salt of his sweat is leaven forever

The bread is abused by tyrants of the house
House of old and newer agonies

It is a tale of the lost basket of foods
The owner and the basket miss each other on the way

And all the tyrants pass for princes today
They wear his name like the crucifix abused

And it is a song of the great merchandisers
God flowers in all their vacuous mouths
But blizzard and sandstorm rage in their hearts

The dance of the tyrants is an evil carnival
Acolytes and drummers are in waves and phalanxes

And thunder comes in a parade of hammers
Seeking the heads of the weak and helpless

They miss the great lessons of all calloused hands
Those who did not break rock by the sea

Those who did not hear the water on the rocks
Those who gave neither rag nor robe
Not even a nuptial for the pity of lepers

The nights are dark and the skies are dark
But their gates are open for revel and carousal

*Ritual animal*
*Gift of the spirits*

Now the cold rock has no more sound
No more fires from the sparks of flint

No more show of dolphins in the air

The fireworks rest in the prisons of fire

It is a grand masquerade of great killer whales
And tyrant's pets are snarling hammerheads

3

*Ritual animal*
*Gift of the spirits*

The world learns only in snatches of agony
But quickly forgotten are all pains of fire

The world is in love with the show of dolphins
Even when the dolphins have no sea to swim

Let smoke waft from the hearths of roses
And thunders rock from the prison stones

The world learns slowly and quickly forgets
The great differences in the gaits of animals

Some will wander like the leaves in cyclones
And some will saunter in the freedom of the air

But the gift of spirits belongs to the village
And no one will kill what the gods will not eat

And the ritual animal walks from farm to farm
Feeding out of what the gods leave for the people

No one will touch a ritual animal
Without the killing glove and cleaver of the gods

4

And so they left the heart of Mandela
With a 46664 holy blazon

It blazed long there in Robben Island
It was a grand meteor stilled in the sky

An electric thing confined without bounds
Inside and above that prison of fire

And there was no hurry in the breaking of stones
The demons which drove the captors knew that

Its memory roams like a rain bearing wind
A totem loaded with the grace of the spirits

*Ritual animal*
*Gift of the spirits*

The village farm and all the crops there are his
To gaze at or graze to his heart's content

*No one will touch a ritual animal*
*Without the killing glove and cleaver of the gods.*

# Ancestral Whispers and a Farm of Flowers (*for Oprah Winfrey*)

How many pick up the whispers of the great ancestors
And walk on like a thief from the barking of dogs
How many pass by the decrepit neighborhood
And think of the souls who roll in hunger there on their mats
How many remember the unsung agonies of those deep waters
Where the bones of slaves roll with the expired throb of time
And how many contemplate the price paid by the living today
For ancestral errors in which they played no part
Deep deep inside our great prisons of fire
The embers of comfort do not make for deep reflections
The glow is too sweet for any windows of freedom
The pulp of comfort tastes best without distractions

Not with you dear sister Oprah
With all the music of all the clouds droning in your ears
And with the weight of all the ivory on your ankles

And with stars twinkling a stable halo around your face
The oldest agonies still bloom sadly in your heart
Forgotten dirges rise to you from derelict crypts
Where precious souls cry for denied memorials
Their wails beat the murmurs of the silent seas
But silences will hide blood in the brine of fresh water
But water will remain the dread memorial for the hot tears
Shed with the blood from the greed of predators
You who have tasted the blood of deprivations
Know better than to be distracted by divisive cries
For division always seals the cracks of freedom
Within the flaming agonies in a prison of fire

Those who do not understand pain cannot understand
The hurrying footsteps and the cries of those who do
They will mount their lame horses of sophistry
And run round in circles of pathetic wisdom
It is never for them a time of sorrow
And never ever for them a time of lamentation
The world is good and beautiful as it is
Beautiful even when there is a carnival of mourning
Ringing many hearts from sunrise to sunset
In the hearts of those who watch hearses of the unknown
The coffins are indeed mere bundles of wood
Like the numbers which commanders-in-chief
Spin out in that strange and lunatic arrogance

When an army is wilting from numbers of the dead

I salute you dear Oprah  forever and ever
For remembering the deathless candles across the Atlantic
Those faintest lights in all our survivors' hearts
For remembering the blood of all the unsung souls
Whose agonies break on the beachsands of two continents
Victims of ancestral errors in the wind of alien greed

I salute you whose sights roved beyond the Sahara
Beyond the mirages of African sands and suffering
Down down into the deep veldts of Southern Africa
Where compassion raised the great diamond obelisk
Which only few can even without sight still sense and feel
The thing which marks blackness as kin of all forgiving
I salute you for falling in quick step with the great spirit
For setting into the deep contours of terrible suffering
Your own monument of sweetest compassion

Your wealth and fame may bloom for a hundred years
But dear Oprah, the flowers farmed on your piece of the
veldt
Will live and bloom  in the hearts of millions and millions
Not mere barren beauty and not evanescent fragrance
Great eternal bouquets everlasting in their goodness.

# WARRIOR HEARTS

## **The Covenant** (*for Malcolm X*)

One day we will begin to name boulevards after you
But we must open the X which your name conceals
The deep secrets which only a few want to face

Dirty hands hoist banners of blood over your homestead
And we whisper your name in the summer moments of our lives
The winter agonies want all boulevards named after you
But the great X of your name bears the potholes of death

The boulevards go well with Martin Luther King
He bought our pellet guns from the phony market stalls
The avenging angels armed you with the great whip
They know the language which even the mad understands

Out of our prisons of fire we rode the storm of your blood
And our hearts build asphalt boulevards for you everywhere
We know you shopped for the tools of war in the right stalls
We know if you were wrong, Christ must also be wrong

When the tribes gather at the final roll call of the ancestors
We will all remember how your hand reached out for love

Across the oceans to Africa and the rest of the world
From prince of black anger you turned prince of black love
Your name will shake the heavens in great bull thunders
Your tears the diamond studs on our crowns of peace

The gospels will repeat what our hearts have always
known
Christ left the whip there in the holy vestibule for you
After his cleansing of the temple and the flight of gamblers
Before X became part of the great covenant of our race...

# **Invocation** (*for Che Guevera*)

Teach me to know through the people
To look into the wells of the eyes of the people

Into the eyes of man and of woman and of children
To shudder at suffering and not at death's ugly face

To remember all the ugliness which lurk deep down
Down down the wells which deprivation digs always

Teach me to know death through the people
To lift my heart and its agonies like a shield

Between the powers of deprivation and destruction
I will stand there like the iroko tree in the wind

I will be the great staff of the people's medicine
The breath of power from the passion of the people

I will always listen to the breeze in the evening
When all things are quiet like the heart of the helpless

I will speak only in the timbre of true heroes

Teach me to know always the face of my own death

To know my pain only through the pulse of the people
For my breath of power to be the passion of the people . . .

# Desert Wind *(for Gaddafi)*

Those who call themselves gods always live in fear
Somebody has told them in daylight that they are not gods

They may know the blizzard but do not know the sirocco
But the world cannot be ruled by the king with one eye

Thanks for whatever makes elephants trunks pause and halt
Whether it is desert wind or the glare from a hero's face

Like the animals in the wild at the spoor of lions
Those gods fear the great gaze of steel like they fear the night

They know at what age you buckled the knees of elephants
Their ears have tasted the sound in the crash of elephants

They know that they have the limbs of elephants
And they know they should fear all elephant hunters

And so they fear you as they fear all leaders of the hunt
Pity who always call themselves gods in their fears

I salute those whose names cause the tremble of elephants
The true gods are those who live as leaders of the hunt

The elephants sweat and tremble in their nightmares
They dream of the cool hearts of the leaders of the hunt

# No Sunset for Heroes

## (*for Fidel Castro*)

The greedy among us are full of lamentation
Their tears are for what they cannot taste before the sunset

How can they think of the man without a home?
The woman of the lonely parturition cry
The child who has no memory of smiles

How can they think of the sorrows of true heroes?
Those who declare the demons of the people their own demons

*Ah ... Fidel*
*You who declared the demons of the people your own demons*
*When the sunset opens for you its great gate and shuts it*
*Your long shadow will forever be remembered*

Far away in Angola where demons stabbed the big heart of Africa

The pounding footsteps of heroes will be remembered

You came running into the storm of storms
Your footsteps still ring in Africa's ears
Unafraid of the wild denizens of alien vultures and strange hyenas
It was an orgy of death and his royal scavengers
Death was a giant but you called death an ant
And the people stood behind your heart of heroes

The songs of your exploits will ring those shores forever
The memory of you and your heroes is for ever a bonfire
No time of cold will have any legs before it

Festivals do not forget the names of heroes
Your heart of steel will remain the shield of nightmares

But the greedy among us are full of lamentation
Their tears are for what they cannot taste before the sunset

*Ah ... Fidel*
*You who declared the demons of the people your own demons*
*When the sunset opens for you its great gate and shuts it*
*Your long shadow will forever be remembered . . .*

# Simple Steps

## *(for Samora Machel, Julius Nyerere, and Thomas Sankara)*

I salute you who saw the mirrors behind the gold flakes of smoke
I salute you who heard the devils quaking the earth and stood your ground
I salute you who knew too well about the burial of the kings and queens
Their golden chariots and special jets have no room in the narrow tomb

This is the great era of vacuous memories and of empty visions
We live in times the tarmac cuts through the shrines of our fathers
We live in times deluges hide the embankments from the lake edge
Times when the very ground is robed in films of treachery
We live in times without memories of our gods or goddesses
Times when we do not understand the holy language of the big gods

Times of blood and greed and greed and blood
And the flags you wove out of your tendons of steel mean nothing
We live in times when the teachers can no longer tell or know
When the headhunters and the people's stalwarts are singing one song
When daylight is heavy with the robe of the deepest nights
When the blind man is happy with his cane in the hands of mad people

The gamblers are shaking with carousals deep hours of worship
Because they know that their congregations are wrapped in soporific mists
Today's incense is for worship but not for the old gods of your hearts
Incense is today for the great golden deities of the alien wilderness
We are inspired by the desire to forget the bleeding heart of the land
We are inspired to treasure the desert storm of our peoples suffering
We are inspired to think of today as the very end of all days
We are inspired to believe that the planet is dead matter

only
The spirits of the ancestors live in the howl of the alien wilderness
The great colonnade of *ogilisi* trees ends in the black hole of creation

Some remember your simple steps in their solitary dreams
Remember you when the dykes of the heart can no longer hold their agonies
Some remember your simple steps in the nightmares driven by our woes
Remember you in the evenings when long nights are awaited in fear

You who saw the meaning of life in the happiness of the people
And let the drums of praise singers beat into the alien wilderness
Who does not remember you is in league with the harmattan devils
The harbingers of drought and famine and dreaded diseases
With the monsters who parch the people's souls in the season of rains
Is in league with what robs the soul of the leaders the will of the gods

What removes from our troubled spirits the faintest of
lights and sights?

You who saw the phony gold flakes dancing before the
smoky mirrors
You did not bow to either the magic of the people or to
alien magic
I salute you for making the brave choice of the stalwarts of
the people
You could tell deceit like a great general could read the
tides of war
You made your call with the deep wisdom of the great an-
cestors
Golden chariots and special jets have no room in our nar-
row tombs
Not even for the burial of kings and queens and all their
royal brood
Royalty who strode around the clan with the simple steps
of commoners
I salute you for planting your wisdom in the souls of the
people . . .

# Burning Bush

## (*for Christopher Okigbo, with oja flute and a slow Atilogwu orchestra*)

1

The Okpatu hills tremble in my dreams
The drapery of green has turned ochre

Our prison walls of hatred and pain
Explode over the shoulders of the hills

Stifled groans echo your death now
The hills and our hearts suppress something

Like our horizon of strange dark clouds
Where the python of hope heaves in distress

*Christopher! Warrior poet!*
Blessed with the power of the water of Idoto

I smell your angry blood in the bush fires
The hills writhe with your wasted passion

And without shame and without remorse
Without the fear of the silence of the groves

Idiots step over your mantle of blood
As they do over the legs of morons

*Christopher! Warrior poet!*
Surrender the magic of the empty scabbard

At the point where thunder kissed your cheek
And all the oracles spilled hallowed satchels

When you speak with Chukwuma Nzeogwu
Tell him that jackals are now in the grove

Virgin fronds, egg shells, fingers of chalk
All is dust and blinding smithereens

Tell him they have stolen the magic of the mask
And robbers now play diviners and carvers

*Tell him our world is now a pitiful weakling*!
*It groans with the burden of an elephant corpse!*

2

*Christopher! Warrior poet!*
*Dike ji ofo jide ogu*! Like the ancestors

You read the goddess book of war and blood
That war and blood are the blights of flowers

That poison could be the wine of honor
The holy water of the garden of sweets

When jackals stomp into the sacred groves
To begin a parade of wild animals

*Christopher!* It is now a parade of wild animals
It is a season of wailing souls, *ugulu di egwu!*

Terror mounts sentry at the gates of sleep
It is a season of wailing souls, *echi di ime!*

These days are nightmares of iron hoofs
With nights of flint and red coals of pain

It is a deep night of wailing souls, *abani di egwu!*
A season of the terror of knotted things

How all bear the sermons of jackals

Of mongrels glowering over starving babies

It is a season of beastly inaugurals
Of red fangs and growls and howls of blood

A yellow fox sits on a trumped gold throne
Surrounded by hyenas in scarlet cassocks

It is a carnival of stolen red caps
And of eagle feathers mixed with chicken feathers

Of beaded crowns from ancient nightmares
Of clowns pulsing with poisoned daggers

Resplendent rogue angels in gold on white
Scornful of detection scornful of law
Because the air is ruled by a king of thieves
In brazen majesty from barns to groves

It is a carnival of such giddy heights
A risen Jadum will cry for another death

Such saccharine chants such cheap magic
Lace the air with soporific pain

With mass agony in sweet refinement

With murderers and swindlers clinking glasses

Chalices chalices in a smell of blood
With people's pain elixir! Elixir!

*Christopher! Warrior poet!*
I tell you again. It is a parade of wild animals

*Our world is now a pitiful weakling*
*It groans with the burden of an elephant corpse*!

3

Listen. The flute plays. The flute plays
It plays for the mask of a thousand mirrors

The palms are swaying means that all is well
The bole is well is why the iroko stands

The green grass glistens on Okpatu hills
And there is no storm there on the Great River

But listen again to the wailing of the flute
For each dancer in the streets a secret spirit piper

A pointing child is never a wild waif
Something lurks there at the fingers end

And when the toad dances in bright broad noon
Spirits of evil are drumming somewhere

*Christopher! Warrior poet!*
The flute plays. Listen to the flute. The flute plays

It is for the mask of a thousand mirrors
They are still calling the mask the elephant

Restrained by wild-eyed drunk acolytes
A mask of a thousand mirrors stomps the streets

*Christopher !* This mask still answers the elephant call
But this mask now lives in the palace of the king

The web of mystery is wet and cold
A bulldozer sits now over the great ant-hole

With gold and guns and terror bearers
Standing over where the spiders wove

The flutes wail aloud for the true great mask
The dance of this mask is a tale of memories

A tale of women octogenarian

A tale of old men serene with suffering

A tale of thunders without a sound
A tale of the earth without an axis

*Christopher ! Warrior poet !*
That stomp of elephants is a phony stomp

*Our world is now a pitiful weakling*
*It groans with the burden of an elephant corpse !*

4

Listen again now. There is a commotion of drums
It is not about war or our cries of pain

It is not about sickness or our deaths like flies
It is all about the sharing of meat

*Listen Christopher to a commotion of drums*
*Of cleavers and pitch forks and of longest knives*

*It is a great rumble of the feast of clowns*
*With Obiako Nchoncho riding on the wings of thunder*

*In a crown heavy with stolen gold and diamonds*
*Trailed by a serenade of blind mad men*

*His burning big eyes greedy red like coals of fire*
*And iron-fanged teeth stained with the blood of innocents*

*With demon robber armies roaring salvation anthems*
*The return of avenging angels and of phony deities*

*Aware of the weakness of the hearts of the wailing masses*
*Desperate for the reedy crutch and the wispiest straws*

*The Nigers incarnates are there from the deep waters*
*Monsters exiled by the wrath of the river goddess*

*They will sell mothers and they will kill babies*
*They will scoff at the sun and the moon and the stars*

*They will make music on the floods of sorrow*
*Over crumbling homesteads weedy pathways*

*Over passageways flaming with dis-ease*
*Over passageways of marbled ignorance*

*It is a joust of giant palace robbers*
*Pitching wiles against their clones in the streets*

*Christopher ! Warrior poet !*
Blessed with the power of the water of Idoto

The bush burns over the Okpatu hills
But the rodents of evil dance unscorchable

I thrive in the smell of your angry blood
Writhing with the passion of the burning bush

It is a strange grave prison of fire
Without hawks and kites without head-hunters

Listen Christopher to our commotion of drums
The voice of the wind playing to empty scabbards

Where the old flute plays like a midnight wail
For the ears of the restless and the abandoned dead

Do tell the ancestors of the elephant stomp
The whole criss-cross and the call of clowns

Tell and tell all the crowned fire-bearers
Tell Chukwuma Nzeogwu and his band of true angels

It is a world of stunning white vultures
Sailing in grace and eerie resplendence

It is a world of laughing hyenas
Redolent in mirth freedom without bounds

Again a parade of wild animals

Growling aloud for a thunder carnival

*Christopher ! Warrior poet !*
The flutes play loud with a commotion of drums

And the great mask answers the elephant call
But it is a theater of very strange shadows

Masks over men and men over masks
The wail of women in demon parturitions

With babies lost in daily dragon dreams
Where the python locks sunset and sunrise

In a twist of things beyond all medicines
Beyond the sun's eye and the smile of moons

*Christopher ! Warrior poet !*
*Blessed with the power of the water of Idoto*

*I cry for the albumen of yellow virgin fronds*
*For this prison of fire and unnameable steam*

*Our world is now a pitiful weakling*
*It groans with the burden of an elephant corpse!*

# The Crucifixion

## (*for Robert Mugabe*)

1

There is a new moon of blatant denials
The moon of mountains of fabrications

From rafters of hamlets to skyscrapers crowns
Voices of denials, voices of fabrications

The smiths have placed a cross on calvary
A cross of iron glowing red with fire

They did not take the son of God's denial
They took the word of their cloned witnesses

For Judas must hurry to marry Barabas
For the doxology of equal peoples

And there will always be cloned witnesses
For the sacred visions of all holy robbers

And they will parade like God's own truth
With angels feathers the masters largesse

Cloned witnesses come with prophecies
With Barabas floating on whispers of pity

Prophets have already seen the crucifixion
So how can the masses miss the resurrection?

2

They presented two thieves to Pontius Pilate
Resplendent Barabas beside a naked Christ

A Pilate who cares little about bleeding heads
And agony from a thousand crowns of thorns

From the rains of stones at the heads of innocents
From the wails of women wilting in sorrow

Pilate accepts the thrill of secret suffering
Like the private agony of a burning moth
Pilate sees children's faces dazed with fear
They are staring into an expiring sun

Their futures are branded with a flaming *Z*

Years of yellow horror with no hope of rain

But Pilate will not speak unless the masters will
One ghostly nod will be fine command

But Pilate understands the hearts of plaintiffs
And the thundering eloquence of the silent birthmark

Children live through life like prison sentences
The sins of parenting are their inheritance

What else do we need for a prison of fire?
Beyond the agony of a blank horizon

A blind people thronging to a cross on calvary
Driven by a smell of blood like angry sharks

A people with barren memory and a taste for misery
A leashed unstable fury fired by slavers' ghosts

For there was already a burial in every heart
With the cry of the chosen thief in silent seas

So many eyes with faces glued to heaven
With a raging prison of fire built long ago

Long before they heard the name of Barabas
Barabas...A name floating on whispers of pity

Give me obsequies. Give me the Christ
Obsequies for the death of imagined thieves

And in the horizons of their wicked dreams
A twin of lurid rainbows grace the sky

Incarnate of the python's beauty
It is a mirror of hearts flushed with red desires...

3

Those who throng to the cross are wise
But they have also lost their memories

Those who now clutch stones of freedom
They were not there with the Christ in the temple

With guilty gamblers fleeing in terror
When the whips of Christ smacked their evil hearts

They did not hear the phony loud wails
With which the pharisees tormented their parents

The gamblers knew well the temple owners
They knew the final limits of their guile

And about Gethsemane the mob knew little
How can one see the mountain top from a deep valley?

The mob knows little with their clutched stones
About the long nights of sorrow in Gethsemane

The syllables of pain from the cross of blood
The scalding spit of the vengeful sadists

About the lashes and the agony on the cross
About the long road of stone to Calvary...

4

Ignorance rides on active white geldings
In the empty rooms of muddled heads

And there is a special Judas battalion
Banners in billows with thunder as usher

They know about the prisons of fire
Roaring in the distant regions of the heart

But the din of their folly is a mighty ocean
The waves are one with the active white geldings...

5

Barabas. Barabas. Barabas.
His name floats on whispers of pity

To rob a poor mute widow will not count
To rob a holy temple or a sacred grove

The big thieves must rob from all the gods
And hold as trophy their sacred genitals

Whispers of pity. Whispers of pity
There is no alcohol in the blood of Barabas

The blood of Christ is the opium water brew
The galaxies cannot stand its ethereal thrust

Beyond Barabas and whispers of pity
Whispers of pity. Evanescent steam...

6

Army of salvation angels
Soldiers of the sacred truth

The masters took Christ to Pontius Pilate
The sins of Barabas did not need the dock

But one cross only glows red on calvary
A cross of iron with clear dimensions

And you only whisper the name of Barabas
Barabas. Barabas floats on whispers of pity

And the blood of Barabas is like tepid water
It will not salve our thirst for joy

It will inflame our prisons of fire
It will not douse one bonfire of evil

The blood of Christ is the glycerine thunder
The miracle of our broken bones of hate

The blood of Christ is the panacea of evil
Detergent and iron scrub of all our woes

The blood of Christ is the final semaphore
Flagging us straight into heavensgate

But they will not whisper the name of Barabas

It is a long stony road to heaven

Barabas. Barabas. Barabas.
His name floats on whispers of pity...

7

A cross glows red on calvary
Another little rib will help prop it there

The horizon crackles with a million tips of fire
It is the exodus from a millennium of bondage

But the march of freedom is a stillborn birth
The virgins flee from the pain of parturition

The cross on calvary is an iron cross
The council of smiths met before the thief was born

The virgins know of the slavers bellows
What embers stoked the heat for the iron

The virgins will not give a holy chastity
To wild gangs of fucking brutish angels

To eunuchs from nightmares of devil harems

To impotent gigolos drunk with synthetic aphrodisiacs

8

Let those who are announcing the resurrection
Lead us to the quarry where stones are broken

Let those who are announcing the resurrection
Lead us to the white glory of the pickets rendezvous

Let those who are announcing the resurrection
Lead us through the magic of the sacred grave

Let those who are announcing the resurrection
Lead us to where Barabas stands naked with Christ

Let those who are announcing the resurrection
Lead us through the history of all the crimes

Let those who are announcing the resurrection
Lead us through courses in slick ventriloquy

Lead us through the evil chambers of secret services
Where crimes of oppression are sacralized by greed

To where the big yam is a glowing tantalus

And the knives of murderers are chosen priestly tools

Lead us through the cabals of the big powers
Where deep nights are designed for smaller peoples

To where all the lights of comfort are shared
According to how one submits to the thongs of bondage

Lead us through all the evils of cartography
The cartography of conquered lands and all souls

Of man and woman and all people in a rainbow
To where the gods designed genitalia from flowers

Before the conclave of sartorial geniuses
Where all the clothes of Barabas are designed

Before the experts of plastics and prosthesis
Where they designed the ultimate images of pity

Before the announcements of the great resurrection
Before the strange, court before Pontius Pilate

Where Judas marries Barabas in a nuptial of stars
And doxology mixes with whispers of pity

And the chosen thief becomes the guilty thief
In a thunder of approval from all the cosmos...

# Master of Fires

## (for *Nnamdi Azikiwe*)

*The story was that the great statesman, octogenarian weak, was often found pacing the balconies of his Onuiyi Haven at nights, mumbling to himself about the tragedy of the great country he had helped to birth : "Is this what we fought for or what we died for...?" His agony was at its peak in the days of General Babangida's dictatorship during which he once told the Nigerian press regarding his oracular inscrutability and intriguing silence: "you cannot argue with a man with a gun !"*

1

Every land on fire wails for a master of fires
For who will deliver the flood for the dousing

For the voice blessed to check panic like a dyke
For the iroko whose leaves are green and gold

For the thunder which waits like the bait of fishes
While the people pulse for their priming call

In the magic hour of the saving new birth
When the hour of a hunt heaves like a sealed second

And the eagle of the homestead perches without armor
And red-eyed hunters rush through groves in droves

And the heart of the eagle waits for one stray bullet
One stray bullet from a drunkard or a maniac

For what will work like the medicine of labor
When to fail spells the ceremony of death

When abandoned gods wail for a thousand second burials
For whatever will suffice for the totems without rituals

When forest and highway tremble for a master of fires
To tell the smoke of incense from bush fire smoke

2

Nnamdi Azikiwe: I hear your midnight voice again
Your grey laments from the parapets at Onuiyi

Is this what we fought for and is that what we died for?
Nnamdi Azikiwe: your memory hunts my heart and head

The fire and smoke billows from horizon to horizon
That is not what you fought for, not what you died for

Like a jewel burnished in the hands of a smith
You returned after ranging over clouds and skies

The pride of the people in the eyes of aliens
Rare elixir of the bitterest of agonies

Heavens' safe armor made you a totem of the people
And safe from alien guile and safe from alien gun

Distant hills echo your cry from the parapets
Distant hearts today repeat your midnight agonies

Those who knew you cry like those who do not
Because the years have rolled their agonies into one

One stony burden heavy like a great ukwa fruit
Uncertain menace hanging over a village footpath

3

Nnamdi Azikiwe: for those farms you left
A flaming bush is what waits in its stead

Fat predators hunt for souls of the burning bush
And nothing in the silences baffle their eagle eyes

You would have corralled the mad arsonists
The thieves who claim cross and ruddy crescent

And hear the thundering voices of famished children
The sorrowing sick trailing after trundling trash bins

Closed school rooms housing screeching mice and lizard
Hospitals where smell of death is the comfort of the sick

And streets and highways teem with death's sentinels
Smiling from potholes the sudden unmarked abyss

In a wild world where a hallowed constancy
Belongs to hazard and death in mean sad doses

4

Nnamdi Azikiwe: there is laughter in the streets
It is the laughter of thieves and of shameless poachers

Saccharine liaisons of tyrants and monsters

The pleasure in their swaggers is from memory of loot
The invitations for those who fear for what follows

Should the barn owners return with trenchant machetes
Blessed and ordained by the spirits of vengeance

Should the village squares regain their lost memories
With a red resurrection of fiery wicked ghosts

Should the great buzz of bees after your great name
Join the fearsome darkness of your old vanguard

In the silent graveyards of immeasurable sacrifices
Pulsing with the pain of a world without totems

5

Nnamdi Azikiwe: your name evokes a memory of tears
When tears meant something with deep roots in dreams

Inside the silences of the fires of oppression
Inside the chambers of the great wait of the mind

At the door of that moment of the great presage
When chains of evil prepare to clatter down

Into the chagrinned plate of the beaten master
Unaware of the tethered energy of the charged interlude

When the air is primed in the great readiness
Flagging off dolor for a breeze of flowers

The great blue lightning of an expectant thunder
The knife of the serration for the drawing of blood

To water the famished farm of all my people
Not saline tears released from pent up wails

The thundering waterfall of a cleansing bath
A noose of steel on an ugly nations neck

The heave needed to drop and explode
The load of the agonies from the idiot monsters

Whose worlds are wrapped with strange carnal comfort
From the great blindness in the waltzing with death

6

For one season of the confluence of wit and ideas
Nnamdi Azikiwe ; conjurer of peace from inflammable tinders

I will follow you into the grey zone behind the deep dances

The zone of grey feared by the arsonists' hearts
The zone of the chalkways of the great ancestors
The great path of bones marked by *ogilisi* trees
Where the robbers of their people have no hiding room
Where charlatans have no chances in the fields of light
Where the master of fires wins tapers from the spirits

I will follow you into the grey zone behind the deep dances
Where all tribes gather at the foot of the master of fires
Where the true stalwarts are practicing the credo of new times
Where the dour tale of the vulture against the royal eagle
Has turned into the tale of the eagle and the tale of the vulture
Where each bird knows the tale of each for one branch
Against the liaison of tyrants and of idiot monsters
Where leaderless homesteads tremble in a storm of mongrels
And satanic breeds bray for grass like crazed horses

With pale pacific hearts wailing for a master of fires
In a ceaseless season of howls and of snarls

I will follow you into the grey zone behind the deep dances
Beyond the dark windows of sweaty nightmares

Where your vanguard rules alive with rising sun glory
Where your words mutate into millions of angry people
Where the world pauses to watch the spell of your thoughts
Content to revel in the soaring crest of your dreams
At the great confluence of wits and of ideas
Buzzing the great zee of your infectious power
Angry millions on the march for the thrones of tyrants
Angry millions answering to the call of thunder
Restless angry millions screaming for the throats of tyrants
Screaming at the wicked ways of the idiot monsters
Screaming at the strange liaison between the devil and power
*Is this what we fought for or what we died for?*
*Is this what we died for or what we fought for?*
*Is this what we fought for or what we died for?*
Angry millions alive joined by angry millions of ghosts...

# Looking Back in Anger, Dear Patrice (*for Patrice Lumumba*)

Some of us may look back in anger, Dear Patrice
When the winds of regret howl over the *ogilisi* trees
And the alien blood merchants define themselves
In the lines of misery all over the land

See what horror they brought to the people
Those ogres, wild weed, and planted saviours
The harvesters are always the wild eagles
The bats with two homes in the heart of time

And nesting without shame from among us
Those arctic demons insensitive to the heat
They wear their blackness as the badge of deceit
Fooling strangers and tenants in daylight

The poverty of the people will not touch them
The voices of suffering children will not touch them
Nor the plaintive moans of the widows at night
The hyenas from the souls of disembodied pirates
Brazen poachers unashamed by the light of time
Those are their waiting regiments, Dear Patrice
The faces of their ancestors will not halt them

Lovers of broad appian ways of blood and evil
But who on earth can run from ancestral paths?
Lovers of blood will vie and die victims of blood
Goodness is the army of ghouls after them and before them

They cringe and hide from the storms of our prayers
*Oh Gods of all our dear suffering people*
*Protect us from traitors whose hearts are stone*
*With no soft spaces for souls of people who are worthy*
*Ready to die for the people like Patrice Lumumba*

They are still out there prancing among us
Among us always brothers and sisters in hoods
Renegade incarnates and vicious wanderers
Those the ancestors locked out from the great halls
Demon winds against the hardy *ogilisi* trees
They will howl on forever and forever
Dust will be the cornerstone of all their homesteads

They know all the prisons of fire
Their gleeful roles at callous constructions
Of barbed fences over the souls of their clans
But Dear Patrice, forgive them all
Dust will be the cornerstone of all their homesteads
Who choose the rust of iron from the deep souls gold
Who choose dust for the cornerstone of their homesteads...

# What the Sea Washes Back

## (for *Kwame Nkrumah*)

Even if they had buried you far from the Atlantic
Far from the mist and the great beauty of Accra
The world would still hear what the sea washes back
When the breakers offload their agonies on beach sand

The horizon after you looks empty and forlorn
But what one sees hit the senses like magic diamonds
Your glinting thoughts unafraid of the light of time
Drum back from Cairo to the Cape of Good Hope
Those whose ears were loaded with iron and stone
Hear the breakers thundering back your words
And those who knew with you about the great ambush
Of alien lions waiting for the slender deer of Africa's soul
Gnash their teeth in poignant lamentations

It is not lost yet on all those who remain anxious
The kernel of your words which traitors reveled to sully
The mad scramble back for those glinting nuggets
Is good sign that what the ancestors planted with diligence
Cannot just wilt from the gust of idiot winds
*Wisdom is hardy like our great Iroko trees*
*It is the great baobab in the deep night of rogues*
Your words will remain like the forest of Iroko

Far from what breakers smash back on beachsand

Light comes from the buried agonies of all ancestral giants
The pall of time and the din of idiot winds
Will die like the carousals of fools in the morning
After their clowning drummers and pipers are on wings
From the lights from the eagle eyes of great heroes
The eyes of those who stare into the eyes of cowards
Hiding behind the mask of the brutish in us
Those who content their hearts with a moments fireflies
And still contemplate the sale of their mothers

The days of lamentation will not be long
The sandy beach will soon tire from the breakers of your soul
And the old agonies will flake off with the wind
And the wails of all the calloused ancestors
Will touch and soften the hearts of all progenies
And they will begin to reconsider the haste of the stupid farmers
Those who stood up to dig for the yam of your thoughts
Who today must kneel with the diligence of the great ancestors
And search for the damaged tubers which the barns did not keep
With all those things which should nourish our limbs
When alien lions roar for the flesh of the clan...

# SQUINTS FROM THE PRISON IN THE HEART

# From a Competing God:
# The Sharks Are Not There

## (*for George Bush*)

(*Responding to a little girl who asked me what I think of God and the world with so much violence and suffering everywhere... This was during a discussion with her mother in the most brutal, ugly, thunderous and unearthly "shock and awe" phase of the war to change the regime of Saddam Hussein in Iraq* )

1

I am the poet of the fish bowl
I am no ordinary poet

I till silently the earth of my dreams
Murmurs are refrains in the axes of my plot
The golden bridges of a world of differences

I planted the fish as I planted all things
Those with roots and those without roots
And I wrote the sharks out of the beauty of the farm

And it is a bowl of variegated lives
And the sharks are not there

Those who race to the smell of blood
They are just not there

The electric fish is there
Fish with hidden poison
Fish with tentacles of death
Wild octopal horrors
Horned things with candelabra heads
Unicorned snouties and the pincer-limbed
The spotted and bat-like
The turtled and the ancient-mailed
Quilled like the porcupine or maned like the lion
Most weapons are honed for nothing but show
And the sharks in them are not there
The sharks are just not there

2

I know the glory of the power of making
I fear the glory and the power of making
The spirit of the glory and the power of making

I love this world of nudges and kisses
I love the thrill of making for pleasure
Like the noise of swimmers when they float for fun
I love this world of nudges and kisses
Birds floating against the blue of the sky
Raising visions nursed from the frolics in the bowl
I love this world of nudges and kisses
Among the fine pebbles and the silver sand

And the sharks are not there
Among the weed and fern and palm and grass
And the sharks are not there
Among sea vegetation variegated as the lives
And the sharks are not there

3

It is a world of nudges and of tender kisses
For fish in chase and fish at the horizons of glass
Of fish in the middle and fish in the bottom
And who knows what they make of things
Of the weeds and fern and palm and grass
It is a world of nudges and of tender kisses
Among the fine pebbles and the silver sand

What do they know of their horizons of glass
What plans I have for my Disney of pleasure

My world of grace and dreams without bluster
I made it for them to see beauty in the day
And for them too to see beauty at night

I made it for them a world for kisses
A world of nudges and a killing-less world
I made it for them to keep their poisons for food
For the tentacles of death for the desperate moment

Wavelets move the weeds with the fishes there
The silver sand ruffles and settles down
All is rolling with the music of the water
The fishes play in nudges and in kisses
Among their harmless guns of bubbles

Among the weed and fern and palm and grass
Among little stones and pebbles without edges
Among things that cannot be missile
All sleep as I sleep without nightmares
The sharks are not there at all

Monsters too are not there at all
With my words, I write them out with the sharks
Monsters live only in their prisons of fire
For those who race to the smell of blood are not there
The sharks, my friend, are not just there...

# Of Tales and Broken Columns

(*for Tony Blair*)

1

The galleys of blood docked long ago, sir
No more wind to give the sails ballast

The mariners are new sir and so their horizons
This world is now too sober for tales

The pirates and their loot have walked into the night
Light picks up the grain of sand on the peopled beaches

It is a finite quest for the glory in flowers
In the beauty lost in our gory appetites

2

If the temple of the heart is clean and open
Emperors learn from the walls of old empires

Robed in moss, the broken columns are there always

It is a scraggy bush of rats and of happy lizards

Like us too chirpy birds visit the dead birds there
The tired floors echo their droppings and the past

Whispered by the wind the old tales are there
But the ears of this world are too sober and keen

3

Tales of a resurrection may weave a new blindfold
Yet no one else will be knighted today

No, not for blood and not for swash-buckling
When bags of tricks wait at the open-market stalls

Magic is no longer now for the great mages
Rain falls from the old darkness of the clouds

Rain falls too from a heaven of white clouds
Mastery will always come with time

4

The world of today is too sober for tales
The tales are too heavy for our trundling hearts

The horizon is not an old gate to the abyss
It is a round world today for fools and sages

Because there is nowhere else for one to go
In the sad dark alleys of our failed visions

And from the white mountains of our hot dreams
This round world is one prison of fire...

5

Somber faces are what the past offers for treasure
Wisdom blazons from old paths of blood

Time sobers the most stubborn among us
No one believes the tales of unicorns

This world of today is too sober for tales
The tales of monsters and of strange alien things

These tales are now like broken columns
The Acropolis of only curious eyes...

# **King David Hotel** (*In Memoriam*: *for Menachan Begin & the Irgun*)

1

Every world comes from a lighting of fires
Our hearts are thonged with their flames of gold
We set a throne in the center of the sky
And the monarch we make wears his noble crown
Fees are not there for the stoking of his radiance

It is now a world of little gods
Their dignity is no great cipher
It is brazen like trumpets in the sun
It is thrust in view like the tongues of snakes
Bold and garish like the ogle of whores
This manner of radiance is not for kings
Clowns may well find there a fitting show
When the blood of others is sewer water

2

Everybody knows that the spigots are obscene
Which soak the green grass on the lawns of power
But the cry of lost tribes is like the beating of wings

And the swishing of trees in an empty homestead
And in this world of very little gods
A word of the dead is still luscious wine
When the word of the dead is not of our own dead
It runs merrily down our busting guts

We have planted a monarch here today
Is what we tell tomorrow's acolytes
All who search for light in the deep night
They will join our singing in our world of gods
This song of David at the gathering of tribes

Who will pause at the song of patriots
When the billowing flag demands only one voice
From the mad ones hiding in the angels' halo

3

We saw the blood you showered here yesterday
We see olive branches sagging today
They sag with fruits no one will taste
Cloned for peace from the big house tree
No one believes the miracle of the blossoms
With the memory of Christ's anger in the wilderness
Because He cursed the fig tree for its barrenness

Many who wait today in their prisons of fire
Feed on the stones of their own anger
Curses will not do for their heads fig trees
They load every breath with dreams of death
Smithing ugly missiles with their own blood

After the rain of blood on perched tongues and throats
The rain must seek what houses the roots
What quickens the agonies in the desert sand...

# HEARTS IN THE WILDERNESS

# Song of the Unknown Soldier

1

So many have fled into the woods today
Because the bugle's call is the call of death
So many have fled into the woods today

I have followed the voice of the earth goddess
Her river breaks up all streaks of blood

She holds the umbrella of the silent ways
The way of the duck at the commotion of hawks

Power does not walk with thunder's heels
The children of the duck learned that long ago

Thunder's heels leave no spoors behind
The laughter of lightning at the pall of night

That is what thunder leaves behind
Sounds of awe and the memory of serrations
That is what thunder leaves behind

2

I have heard the squawk of chickens
I marked like the hawk the eddies of flight

I know ants will not die from dust and noise
And that elephants will not be moved by games

3

I have followed the voice of the earth goddess
Into the path of all the water denizens

Under the umbrella of the silent ways
Into the big room of the water way

Into the calm corridors of the silent power
Into the mute glitter of the golden stool

Into where cleansing is the magic of hearts
And clean majesty goes without giddy colors

Where power mounts the tip of the obelisk
Where the wind of heights is futile in sways

4

The chief calls me from his prison of fire

He hides his agonies in the bugle's call

The mad crowd hangs round his barren table
Playing with cones on the shallows of life

Blood is the only thing their bugle's blow
Each note of the bugle is a dance of cones

The medicine of all soporific brains
The fuel for hearts without horizons

The picture of the world in a thousand shapes
And each crazy shape is a beauty queen

With half drunk clowns on the judge's bench
Monocular mages in the evening of life

Blood is the driver of their heavenly vision
Rarely is the blood the blood of their people

Your blood and my blood and not their blood
Mean merchants touting grimmest agenda

Wrapped in wool and incense dreams
With deities' thrones at the tips of lips

5

Good soldiers know such prisons of fire
Where the scoundrel's mirth is safe in the shade

And passions run in a braid of rivers
Deep under the king's palace walls

The good soldiers hide under the great umbrella
The shade where the goddess repeats her song

Of everlasting wisdom beyond the termite of time
The story of the peace behind the deep dances

Where orbits do not collide with each other
And all the planets gyrate in perfect peace
Singing the great songs of all the great ancestors
Let a million eagles perch with a million kites

*There is enough room under the sun and stars*
*Except for those longing for the land of the dead...*

# Woman of Iraq

I see through the forbidden veil over your sad face
I see through the bars of your sibilant prisons of fire
I see through the darkness of your sighs of lethargy
I see through your passions of a mother's heart in pain
Your memory pangs assail my baffled brain always
As if I live there in the compound of your remembering

I remember you when no one wants to think about you
I remember you in the heat which no thermometer measures
When your loneliness recalls the cry of a startled baby
The baby whose dream was damaged by the drop of a bomb
The smile of flowers stilled by the red flash of a mortar shell
A sweetness punctuated by the whistles of bullets
The fall of shattered glass and the strange kicks of boots on doors
When your agony recalls the lost steps of a soldier child
A soldier whose warm embrace you will never feel again
When your heart shattered like a clay pot on a marble floor
Because a husband whose love you have known like a

house pet
Will never come home again to share the mercies of sunset with you
I remember you in the pictures of the hobbling injured
Whether they hobble on as yours or as your enemy
I remember you in the twisted bodies in the pools of blood
And in all the gory mess and murk they feed us as news
You are a sharp needle of pain when I sit down at table to eat
Because I remember your appetite killed by the news of death

I see you woman of Iraq, when I hear the politicians on television
Explaining to dumb cameras their theories of war and peace
I see you, woman of Iraq, in the count of bodies of the dead
When one side is staking its claim of victory or of resilience
I see you woman of Iraq when the tabled issues are like mere games
Checkers and chess played in the hall of a drunkards dream

Woman of Iraq, seven thousand miles away from my heart
Because I have known desert heat with no hope of cold

water
Because I have had icy handshakes with grimmest death
I can chart with ease the homeless trail of your orphaned laughter
I see the bleak wonder on your veiled face before my eyes
I see its lines of the empty sunrise of tomorrow etched by fear
I see your tears too like cascades of blood from flaming furrows

Woman of Iraq, moaning alone about your lost sons and daughters
Scarred for ever by fear imagined in temples of greed
My heart breaks with your heart like simple twin drums
Beating hopeless pleas to a world drunk with a strange love
Toasting blood in gold chalices with meals of lies in honeyed cakes

# American Woman

*(for Cindy Sheehan)*

I salute you brave American woman
I salute a courage which beats drums in the streets
I salute the courage which fears nothing
Its echoes will travel gustily into the great future of all lands
And every soul will read and hear its gusty melody
I salute you brave American woman
Because the blood of your fallen soldier child
Is the blood of my fallen soldier child
The world will never forget your tears
Because millions feel the heat of tears on your face
The world will never forget your tears

The source and course of your tears cannot be hidden
Except by curses which mark the coward's pedigree
I salute the courage which beats drums in the streets
I salute the hot tears you shed for many people
The world will never forget your tears
I salute the hot tears you shed for all people

I salute you brave American woman
Daylight and darkness are equal fields of play

I salute the courage which does not wait for darkness
It plants nuggets of fire in the deepest nights
I salute the courage which fears neither man nor woman
It finds the potent godhead in simple things
Not in the awe and pomp which people dread
But in the energy of a flame burning in a storm
And in the secret energy of a reed in the wind
I salute the courage which seeks the essence of life
It finds death in a tomorrow which no one can escape
A tomorrow that is not the product of a strange dream
From the heated brains of the greedy and selfish
Is tomorrow billowing from a banner few understand
And is tomorrow the evening at the end of a flower's glory?
I salute the courage which knows the differences
It knows the desert wilderness from any garden of roses
I salute the courage which dares dream from a ring of fire
Your courage will always find water for any prison of fire
Brave American woman: the world will never forget your tears
I salute the courage which beats drums through the streets
Brave American woman: the world will never forget your tears
Your tears, brave American woman, will never be forgotten

# TWISTED HEARTS:

## POEMS TO MARY ELLEN TOMBSTONE

# Masks

They are hiding under the mother of God
Under the shadows of the phony pedestal

Their gloves are soiled by blades of blood
While Mary Mary roll from their torrid tongues

Nerves of steel manage their genuflections
Even with demons as sentry in their hearts

These men of iron have mastered gestures
And only robots can beat their moves of love

All is illusion because all is ceremony
In that land where marionettes have no tears

The Mary Mary chant  is a chant of cheats
Unwary women bite their baits and follow

The road to power lures with lilting serenades
Far and beyond the sweet *udala* tree

Beyond the beats of the great deep dance
The dance of planets and the naked mothers...

# Mary, Mary

## (*after the Christian Virgin Mary*)

They named her well as the mother of God
She fell down low from the blow of grace

She knew that the grace just came to her
Not for her beauty and not for her strength

Her ward she babied with serene majesty
Working and walking with the softest sandals

She knew what hard heels will do to hearts
All hearts are blessed with very little spaces

Her heart knew well the primer of love
The giving of blood for the birth of life

From a thousand roaring prisons of fire
She read the rainbows simple nuptials

The story of the horizons finest jewelry
And its magic robe of light and water

Stories of fire before the green grass grows
Before flowers knock at the gates of love

Her head knew too that it was the stars
Which lit the candles of her royal glow

And so she lives quiet in the hearts of all
Head bowed and humble with her gift

She leaves the thunders of her might her power
For those who wear her borrowed robes

She knows what is wrong when thunder strikes
And leaves in its path a trail of blood

What they do not know whose heels are hard
Who walk without thought over hapless souls

Who live in the pits of roiling dross
Who love to live without the golden showers

*Which the stars spray daily to power the dance*
*The great ceremonies there in the deepest shadows...*

# Dog of Faeces

## *( for Mary Ellen's sister, a boss who was probably deranged by love of power*)

"The faeces-eating dog dies wrapped in the favorite and most familiar smell..."

--- *an Igbo proverb*

Dear dog of faeces loving closed spaces
Lover of stench in closed horizons

Remember the death of the other last dog
His wrapper of fur lit a prison of fire

But he did not feel the smart of soot
And he did not feel the smart of smoke

His funeral dirge was in the horizon
But he did not hear its thunder drums

And his gold sheen fur was all he saw
And all he heard was a call to glory

And the glory was of vengeful forces
Those who stoked his prison of fire

With anger of hurt they did not desire
Firming the bolts of the prison gates

Where dancing flames strummed of heaven
On a golden guitar that wailed of death

Howling beasts were heard from his heart
Their living embers glowed and turned to ash

And dog of faeces loving closed spaces
The coffin's lid slowly lowered over him

And he died in the world he always knew
Walled by that stench with cold horizons...

# Lady of Plastic, Lady of Iron

She came to me with all the demons
In the shallow silence of her measured gaits

She was a product of strange devices
There was nothing in her I could not read

She was as straight as what made her
There was nothing in her I could not read

This lady of plastic, this lady from iron
She was floating on all the swirls of Cologne

But there was nothing in her I could not read
Too far from the funk of the naked mothers

Too far from what the planets echoed
As they followed the beats of the great deep dance

The crackling fires gave her soul away
In her closeness to the bush of ivy and snakes

The great bush of thorns which dogged each step

She made in her heart as the owner of the world

No knowledge in her heart of the great deep dance
Mimed by the planets in the passageways

She was a wanderer like all those hosts
Whose grimaces strained their prison of fire

Lady of plastic, lady from iron
How would her soul ever win release

Her torments ruled over her little talents
Like a guard of famished dogs and lions

Their carnivores eyes must eat all flesh
For the beasts in them to win quietude

Lady lady beyond the deep deep shadows
Your soul is denied so much sweetness

From the great drummers of the coded dances
*Ruling the world from the deepest shadows...*

# To Kill a Queen

She imagined herself a queen when she spoke to me
Benighted demon from a thousand years of darkness
Queened by the master's whip of bygone years
But light in the tiara of a dummy diamond queen
Is thunder's axe in the avenger's heart

And her words of hatred came back to me
It came from the bellows of hundreds of years
But today is too soon for one aged anger
Red in the forge and breathing from the bellows
And I turned slowly to my secret bow of pain
And the quiver came floating into my heart
Into my heart and into my heart
One after the other and into my heart
And the absorbent matter of my angry blood
Rolled her folly into poison balls

Her arrogance was my only precious goad
To break yet again one prison of fire
One after the other in the depths of my heart
And inside my heart I knew what was happening
And what was to come I knew in my heart

And I drew from the quiver of red potencies
And they found the bull's eye of her heart of evil
Roiling the quiet pond of her old agonies
Each syllable was like our season of storms
Held back and released by the hand of gods
Same gods who gave her the fine old pain
Renewed her old stock of alarum and warp

And she turned into Lucifer on his way to earth
Screaming for cleansing from all medicines
And I wept for her and wept for myself
For I was the bowman of a helpless quarry
Armed with all gods' merciless arrows
I knew she was my fawn from that moment on
Her ugly mask bore the mark of the beast
Sharp under her finery and all jewelry
Under the affectation of a sweetness and light
Faked easily under our village square moon
Her murk stood before my indelible gaze
Down to the dreaded bottom of the end of time

I had seen her nakedness and the dross over her soul
A beast in a cage ruling a strange wilderness
Far, far away from the denizen's comfort
Ungainly her wallows in the sea of ignorance
With no single flag where she saw an armada

This pitiful thing who thought her self queen
Was nothing more than an old scorned slut
Armored only by crown of pedigree
This sloven of slovens in  the street of commoners
Taunted by knowing children fleeing from her shadows
In the red districts of a clown's nightmare...

# Woman at the Gate

In a thousand and one portals in the envelope of fire
One prison gate was guarded by a woman
And blind fools rushed for the gold in bubbles
Drumming triumphals into the deep deep dances
With beats sullying the inviolable chalk ways
And they roamed away from all the naked mothers
Who danced with power under the *udala* tree
The power of the gods behind the old deep dance
*Ruling the planets from the deepest shadows...*

She rode like the wind with one song of terror
I am a woman but I am  a man too
*All God's lionesses fell from the sky*
And she sang better than the little bird *nza*
She dared the great spirits to sing a better song
The prize of her soul she offered without thoughts
And all the great spirits sang along with her
And they turned her song into a song of mockery
*All Gods lionesses fell from the sky*

And they claimed her soul before she sang some more
Though she sang a song with barren memory

She did not know the roots of her one song
Nor did she know about the avenger's paths
Those who bore the great sign of the cross
One sign of surrender among many signs
A marker of the gods of the old deep dance
*Ruling the planets from the deepest shadows...*

Who guards a great gate guards it in trust
Guards the gate for the builders of gates
For the secret scorches of the prisons of fire
For what will live on and what will not live
From fires of the forge coded in the dance of mothers
Who danced with power under the *udala* tree
The power of the gods of the old deep dance
*Ruling the planets from the deepest shadows...*

Lioness of God who fell from the sky
The beauty of flowers are deeper than the colors
The water follows the coconut from the roots
Narrow stems juice the great pumpkin fruit
And so much goes into the formation of clouds
Whether the water turns dew or dark thunderstorm
In the beats of the gods of the old deep dance
*Ruling the planets from the deepest shadows...*

## **The Coven** (*for Mary Ellen Tombstone and Mike Grimbrook*)

The witches sit always around Mary Tombstone
She thinks openly she is the mother of God
The witches do not know precisely what she thinks
Their actions for their Mary are unwitting actions
They really make her feel like the mother of God
The men wear headphones plotting with the devil
For dear Mary Tombstone who thinks she is God
And when velvety death comes Mary does not know
The men  off their headphones and smile at the coven
The men had been lying that Mary is a queen
Pretending ever too that she is the mother of God
And poor Mary Tombstone thinking such thoughts
Gets from the coven a coffin for a gift...

# Neutral One

*(for Pontius Pilate and his friend, Dr. Alf Stern)*

Pontius, my friend, Oh Pontius my friend
You looked as though you washed your hands well
But your mask was what fed that strange illusion
For no red wiles can dim a heart of guilt
Ragged windows will cut ugly appian ways
Straight into that great palace of your soul
All things are clear which the debris rain there
The funky detritus of your sly polished smile
Steam into the atmosphere of your narrow narrow world
The windows are covered with steam from your breath
And panting in fear like an animal caged
The walls of your conscience is a prison of fire
Each nail on the palms of the innocent Christ
Is a nail also into your guilt-ridden heart
You heard the distant rage of the demons with the cross
You heard the jangle of nails and the tinkling of the hammers
You know the formations when formations thirst for pain
Your soldiers did not move because your heart did not move

The people will sing forever in their hours of regret
Songs of demons whose hearts throb like your own heart
Beating the great drums of silence and assent
Will know what the people in the streets have always
known
The witness to crime whose finger does not rise
Crowns his silence with the killer's brutal thorns

# The Worlds We Make

## (For Chuma Ijoma)

The worlds we make and what we do
The greed and cowardice and failed dices
Will give earth the ears she does not deserve
Innocent blood which the goddess does not want

The words of the good will ever live there
With weeds of evil where flowers grow
My garden has learnt to endure like a mule
Where the life-giving dew is small and light
Like the little things which one in want knows
Because of the well of light in us
Holding firm against the deep night winds
Against the storm between blood and air

What ears will ever hear those words
Without a blast in its passageways
The devil walked there into this man's heart
Pitched a tent of cactus and bramble
And poor Chuma whose golden heart
Always thirsts for love and fun and peace

And a world where smiles will rule all hearts
Walked into that realm of death by fire

The tale of evil will always sail there
From waters conjured by strange passions
To the burning shores of all desert dreams
Where our madness stoops to drink like lions
Whose preys the day has already made
With the thundering hoofs of a hapless deer...

# In the Wind's Breath

*In the breath of a little wind*
*All things may kiss the dust*
*And the grave becomes the bed*
*Where all lusters sleep*
*Over the chickens rump*
*Gold turns into dust*
*When the chicken sees the moon*
*And all is an army of spirits*

*In the light of the high noon sun*
*The chicken quacks into the wilds*
*Someone has fouled the air*
*Where no one else is in sight*
*And there goes an ungainly run*

*Dear friend of our father*
*Whenever the wind blows*
*Be calm and be calm*
*And be truthful to the world*
*Hold your wrappers over your breasts*
*Give good cover to your nakedness*
*Whether they are feathers of gold*

*Or skirts from the lowly grass*
*Give good cover to your nakedness*
*So much happens in this world*
*In the breath of a little wind…*

# OF LOVE BENIGHTED

# A Wedding Memory

Our carnival laughter has followed the waves
I do not know what the surf left behind
Our carnival laughter has followed the waves

There are no footprints on the beachsand of festival
Rice and confetti have turned into sand
For a rain of gold and tender flowers
There is a muted thunder of iron and cactus

A dream of dew on glistening leaves
Is a boiling nightmare of desert mirages

When demon boatmen rowed away the boat of love
I raised a weak hand and voice in protest

Demon boatmen, alien monsters of my simple heart
Your pennants pointed to a treasure trove in heaven

My hand still hangs in the midair of your departure
My voice is hoarse in the buried breadth of your deafening sirens

The boat of love has left on the calm waves of our carnival laughter
A burning streak, a sliver of fire, a molten lead of pain

Two pale ghosts with no memories of a past
Mountains of phony mails rain from a sterile heaven
A turbulent wind bears shreds of our carnival laughter
Red envelopes of empty promises, one great prison of fire...

# Slouching to Beat a Wife

1

From the womb in the heart
A sturdy resurrection

Into a prison of fire
This sturdy resurrection

It is a demon explosion
From a tomb in the clouds

It comes like an ancestor
With savage acolytes

2

A silent drum is leading
A silent monster slouching

What kingly emergence
Far from the moon glow

This beast on the march
Far from the moon glow

Beyond the sacred tree
Where the women danced

3

A beast on the march
Far from the moon glow

In the prison of fire
Far from the moon glow

In the shade of colonnades
A silent monster slouches

To a wife without life
In the prison of fire

4

Power is on the march
Beyond the sacred tree

Power is an animal
In the prison of fire

A truce of the womb
With the womb in the heart

A sturdy resurrection
From the womb in the heart

5

Blights light memories
Of the sacred avenues

And reason is at large
On flying wild horses

The moon glow is gone
With song of nude mothers

And over the deep dance
Are wild horses stomping

6

For this beast triumphant
A new march is beating

With heaven's lights out
All spirits turn to stone

And the prisons of fire pause
For the demon explosion

A sturdy resurrection
From the womb in the heart

7

In the prison of fire
One husband is the jury

And that jury is the witness
Slouching to the wife

The woman is the convict
In the prison of fire

Where tablets of the laws
Are clenched fists blazing

8

In the dark world of prisons
There are fiery hurricanes

The pulsing wind is heavy
With the kicks of wild horses

Far from the moon glow
The husband is there ready

For the wife without a life
In that prison of fire

9

The husband is at home
In the prison of fire

The ancestor is home
From across the rivers

Far from the moon glow
The animal is home

Beyond the deep dances
Under the *udala* tree

10

Who will drive the engine

Of the great revolution

This sturdy resurrection
This beast triumphant

This slouch and this menace
Thundering to the wife

Crouching without life
In this prison of fire...

# AGAMEVU (*for a useless pad*)

The cold of the wilderness will not precede me home
And no cold will ice the fire of my heart
The traveler will always come back home
Whoever remembers home forsakes exile

The bird caught in a storm high up in the sky
Knows that high noon is not the end of the day

The bole of a river is also a wilderness

If I do not tell you that now that I thrive
In the deep forest of my fiery sufferings
With my guardian spirit back by my side

If I do not tell you that now...now
That my neck bends with my load of pain

If you are the only pad in the deep wide world
With nothing on my head but iron and bramble
Let me snail home with a load of boulders
And dizzy with labor collapse on the way
Let the sweat of my wanderings burn into me

And like a thousand rivulets hot with salt
Let my naked eyes take their scorpion stings
And my skin rive into deltas of pain

And when the people roll the festival drums
Let my homestead be the middle of the road
The playground of lizards and of the poisonous snakes
Where passersby sing and dance without fear
And pour their scorn into one gourd of hatred
For me and all their memories of cowards

May your feces eating dogs bear my sweet name
If I ever accept you again as a shade or pad...

# QUESTIONS

# Why Should I?

*Askance and bemused he looked at me*
*With eyes that have seen myriads of brambles*
*Festooning great flames of his prison of fire*
*Giant flames which only money could fuel*
*He did not see the walls I could see*
*Ringed with walls with only peepholes*
*A world of a dream he alone could read*
*In terms very real in the template of his heart:*

We heard the great opening whistle together
For the race over blood and bones to the stars
Toward the fiery pulsing heart of the sun
Triumphant over brine on welts and sores
I was a bird winging away from the fire

I did not sit there at the roadside with fools
Watching white eagles loop over the rainbow
And staring at flowers under the sun's gold rays
Of thorn and brackish rain, I had no fear
I knew the faint heart and the godforsaken
And I knew where to pitch my sturdy tent
My stalwart heart and muscles of steel

So why should I open my doors today
Open my doors to these wayfarers
Their eyes did not smart from the saline rivulets
They did not know the story of my heels
Tortured by coal fire dances to the stars
They did not feel the knocks of my knuckles
On the iron doors of the devil's barriers
They do not know of tendons and muscles
Which frayed at the crags of dizzying cliffs
Toward the guardian dragons of a brazen sun

If I should just open my doors today
Where is the beauty in the breasting of tapes
The thirsty throat and its rain of cheers
The hallelujah of this sole salvation
So why should I open my doors today?

# QUESTIONS

Our village gate shakes with raps and strains
Groans from the shoulders of a cold cold wind
It feels a long basket of stony questions
Forbidden in weight like cadaver of giants

Who will bear now the virgin fronds of war
Whose silence will touch the shaking deep
Whose smile will move the water goddess
Whose laughter will stop the hiss of snakes
Whose hands will hold the new born baby
Whose voice will stop the errant chieftains
Whose looks will warn Lord Lugard's knights
Whose stare will burst Lord Lugard's tomb
Whose proverbs will lead the wandering people
Whose nod will strike the match of peace
Whose face will wear a halo like the sun

And who will refract the lights of dark glasses
And bury their rays in our forest of evil
And raise asphalt above the deep water
And burn the bush and prune the trees
And lace the air with the lilting flute

And prime the festival drum's mighty boom
Heard only in the evening of honors

Who will wear the red cap with grace
And lower a humble head for his peers
Who knows how to pin the eagle's feather
Because they know how eagles are trapped
Proud of the iroko scaled in daylight
Proud of the diamond look of sweat
Proud of the woman and proud of the child
Proud of the leather walls of all their hearts
Proud of the breathlessness of all distances
Proud of that one who sees the deep water
And knows the long cane comes from the long stick
And leads us to where the ant-hill lies
Toward the blacksmith and the fiery bellows
To the virgin farm of a new beginning
Far away from this prison of fire...

# Quick Tongue of Today

Where is the tendon in the giant's jaw
With the weight to smash the trap of time

Your quick tongue counts today very fast
It beats into air the scudding dark clouds

My tongue is slow and lame today
Times trap holds the tendons firmly

I can only stare at the clouds today
It was quite different yesterday

When my bosom covered a deep universe
And you were secure under the palling blanket

Unaware of the scudding dark clouds
Unaware after the deep thunderstorms ...

# Rumors of Death

These prisons of fire echo with rumors of our death
The rumors are driven by the sights of calluses
The cries for help lost in wind and rainstorm

We will never die because of what lives in these poems
Mirrors from the haunts we tenanted silently
To prepare our flesh for the whips of our masters

We have already felt the warm piss of pain
We have heard the flight of all the master's whip
We have given up a thousand times
Before the execution cries of the blind robber barons
The clowns who hold the yam and wield the knife
The wax in their ears is in lumps of gold
Mined from the village square of their kindred souls

These poachers will not fool us with the ceremonies
The forced applause will one day turn thunder in the morning
Their hunts and probes were over the public land
Their embroidered laces shine with the glints of our tears
Whenever they gather for their shameless carousals

A mad pedigree guffaws at the somber funerals
They scorn calico for the gaudy brocade
Their laughter is a cackle of rotten promises
You can smell the pieces on the highways of death
The thousands of deaths from pain and broken hearts

I see the blood in their flutes of fine wine
The people's blood drip from their meat and fish
Their food is the cadaver of my suffering people
With tombstone flowers for their roses of love

What time it is for the wind of memory
With the maiden's pot shards on the cold hard earth
We will never die because of these pregnant words
Tough words from the tendons of our tough hearts

When the wind plucks at the forest's heartstrings
And thunders touch the hair of secret dust

And your great heart mimics the coming cyclones
Listen to the syllables of these shards of clay

You will find shelter in the coming rainstorm
And lights when the power goes out again
Your smarting eyes will be cleansed of saline tears

Your laughter will pick up its forgotten robes
And the arena of our hearts will be draped for show

Nothing comes before our spirits look windward
Into the deep horizon of the great colonnades

Where the *ogilisi* trees stand still in the wind
Deathless in the poise practiced in the eyes of the gales
Of sandstorm and sand after sandstorm and sand
Slim and hardy and knotted with calluses
But proud like the spirits of the great ancestors...

# Malindidzimu

# **Malindidzimu** (*Call for Rhodes Men*)

Cecil Rhodes knew where to draw the lines
Right across the heart of deep Africa
And what could be better than across the heart
From the beautiful cape to our cradle Cairo

And when he became tired with all his work
When the ancestral spirits turned his dreams to stone
He chose his bed where the ancestors dwelt
Man of valor who does not know other gods
Neither where to sleep nor not to sleep
He chose the bed of the great ancestors
The dwelling place of the greatest spirits

And the great soul of Africa let him be
For the dirge of guns they gave the silences
*Hyate! Hyate!* which the great elders got
They gave him silence as they gave him the land
And the vocal silence buried him deep in the rocks
Perhaps a warning too for all time-travelers

They do not know that rocks look only dead
They share their breaths with all other hosts

Who do not hear their laughter or cries

*Malindidzimu! Malindidzimu!*
How would he whose ears are stuffed with diamonds
Hear the great cries which the wind stores in its throat
The voice of all the great ancestors
*Malindidzimu! Malindidzimu!*

# LONGING FOR HOME

# The Elders are Dead

The elders have warned Death today
Like the dog-eaters of yesterday
Throw the aromatic leaves away
The dog has fled whose meat we await
The pot boils in vain on the fired tripod

Tattered wrappers have no dignity
When the body to the eye is like shriveled fruit
The elders beg today for pieces of offal
Who ate the choice meat yesterday

They are tormented by memories of good wine
Bull-dozers of evil roll over the lion lairs of their wisdom
There are no metal gongs and town-criers today
No sound is strident enough to wake the elders up

# The House of the Chief

Vultures and crows come today for company
My father's house is now an empty house
What shall I do to the walls today?

I hear the footsteps of ghosts on the stairs
My family is no more today what it was yesterday
A barren wind howls through the once great windows

Everybody in the village thinks I am mad
I am mad because I tell them about the prison
They say they do not see or feel the prison walls

I talk of the snakes of stinging smoke
The red– eyed fires of long days and nights
They say they do not see what I see

They tell me there are no prison walls
But I see all the prison lights in their eyes

I weep for their ignorant souls and suffering

I look at the chief's house sitting on the hill

The village huts spread under the house of the chief

I shall take an army to the top of the hill
The vultures and crows will go with me
I shall kill the chief whose house sits on the hill

After the death of the chief and his band of thieves
The villagers will see the fire and all that smoke
Their vision will cure me then of my madness

And the vultures and crows will fly away
And my father's house will be full again
And the winds will leave my windows alone
With no more smoke from the prison of fire...

# Many mansions

Many mansions there in my father's house
Is the song I sang in my wistful dream
My master's house is now my father's house
And my father's house is the house of thieves

The doors are open there for all the elects
Many many mansions in my father's house
My father's house is now the house of thieves

# The Great River Calls Me

The Niger calls me in the dead of night
With all the great spirits in choral laughter
I feel the weights of their heaving bosoms

*The clatter in the air*
*Is of mantles of fire*

There is laughter and there is pain
With pain inside the laughter

The Great River's passion also heaves with them
And the Niger calls me in the dead of night

*Great witness of all the great agonies !*

Your laughter cannot be without the pain
Your mantle, that mantle
Is a mantle of fire

*Because of all our prisons of fire*
*That mantle cannot be but a mantle of fire*

# ORBIT OF LIGHT

# Bird of Distances

*(A Song for Chinua Achebe, celebrating the fiftieth Anniversary of Things Fall Apart)*

1.

Bird of distances and bird of clear visions
Daring cliff edges and all promontories

No peak is dizzying no falls envisioned
Heaven built in the morning the golden walkways

Heaven and the ancestors in the very early morning
Over the great ground plan and the invisible orbit

They gave you the mantle and the great beak of fire
Heaven and the ancestors so early in the morning

They gave you all the tablets of clean diamonds
And you scripted forever what no storms can move

Your orbit is the orbit of all black souls

Scripted on diamonds with the tears of the people

With heaven and the ancestors so early in the morning
Fighting for your soul and the soul of our clan

*Chinualumogu* was the blazon on your shield
What battles have you not seen at the fronts of our blood?

Where great ancestors rose or dropped their shields
You picked up the stories to limber our spirits

Bird of distances bird of clear visions
At war with heaven and all the great ancestors

So early in the morning and into the evening
It was *Chinualumogu,* the blazon on your shield

Guiding us toward the great distances
With heaven and the ancestors in the very early morning

*With the voices of fosterers and of alien monarchs*
*And the din of their calls for the eagle of the clan*
*But the falcon is not an eagle and the eagle not a falcon*
*The people saw the beads trained on the beak of fire*
*And sang out their hearts with the soul of the clan*

*Ugo belu na oji efelugo ! Ugo belu na oji efelugo !*

With that power of the eagle there in the maiden flight...
Responding only to the horizons of the spirits

2.

Great oracles begin work in the halls of the clan
Before the great passageways to other clans and places

The bird of distances begins from a tree in the land
Before ranging through the skies of other alien lands

The flight must end there at the great colonnade
Where the hardy *ogilisi* trees and the great ancestors

Make memorial of orbits for the clan's witnesses
From the village square trees and back to the clan

The bird of distances and the bird of visions
With heaven and the ancestors so early in the morning

Fights in its flight for the clan and the people
Like the great oracle reading the soul of the people

Wearing mantle and the shield and the great blazon
With heaven and the ancestors so early in the morning

Forever the homestead will guard the *ogilisi* trees
Who knows the great path to the grand colonnades?

No path for fosterers and great alien monarchs
A people's oracle will read the soul of the clan

And so the people sang in the noon of the flight
*Ugo belu na oji efelugo ! ugo belu na oji efelugo ! (*chorus
severally)

*The eagle is not a falcon and the falcon is not an eagle*
*Our eagle answers to the orbits in the sky*
*The eagle answers to the inviolable chalkways*
*Not to the calls of fosterers and of alien monarchs*

The only call of the eagle is the call of the clan
The eagle answers to the inviolable chalkways
The power of the eagle stays green from the maiden
flight...
Responding only to the horizons of the spirits

*Ugo belu na oji efelugo ! Ugo belu na oji efelugo* ! (chorus severally)

3

What do we care about the groove of the orbit
Skewered by fosterers and strange alien monarchs

We read their squints and strange masquerades
Each foot of their dances resonate murky intentions

But no visions no views escape the ringed irises
Marked by the ancestors on the inviolable chalkways

*Chinualumogu* pronounces the trenchant steel
And those who see the scabbard shake in their shoes

They fear the bird of visions and the inviolable orbit
They fear the bird and its balances in the storm

They fear the black grace and its duiker's elegance
They fear the spirit energy of its panther's paws

Where the bird of visions perches the marksmen fail
To train their beads as they do   sluggish crows

The thundering beaks of its drumbeat certainty
Plant in all hearts the signature of lighting
In laces and laces which blunt all blades of war
The stories of the flight build great prisons of fire

Prisons of fire with a foundry everlasting
Where new warriors hone great combat blades

Forget the great fosterers and strange alien monarchs
Never ever will they bow to the shining filigrees

The deepest sounds from your great beaks of fire
Never will their ears acknowledge what they hear

They cannot read the blazon on the combat shield
So how can they see the great chalkways of the orbit?

But the diamond tablets of your scripts of fire
Will burn brightest where the warmth matters most

From village squares where all great exploits begin
And in the great depths of the soul of the clan

For no nations blow for the soldiers of their foes
The great battle biggles for victories not theirs

So bird of distances and bird of great visions
Great eagle soaring in great beauty for the clan

The soul of the clan is with you in the orbit
Out there on the great inviolable chalkways
Singing their hearts out as they did in the morning
Aware of the eyes of fosterers and alien monarchs

With all their beads trained on your beak of fire
*Ugo belu na oji efelugo ! Ugo belu na oji efelugo* !( chorus severally)

*The eagle is not a falcon and the falcon is not an eagle*
*Our eagle answers to the orbits in the sky*
*The eagle answers to the inviolable chalkways*
*Not to the calls of fosterers and of alien monarchs*

Fifty years after the shining lights of your wings
The clan still glows in deathless resplendence

With heaven and the ancestors so early in the morning
Fighting forever for you and the clan

The clan follows your visions deep into the horizon
With virgin fronds gold-toned on your beak of fire

With the stars in showers as the eddies of your flight
Chasing that blazon with *chinualumogu* on the shield...

*Ugo belu na oji efelugo ! Ugo belu na oji efelugo*! (chorus severally)